MID-CONTINENT PUBLIC LIBRARY

3 0000 13246

D0088796

UNTOLD

THE NEW ORLEANS 9TH WARD
YOU NEVER KNEW

by
Lynette Norris Wilkinson

Write Creations

Mid-Continent Public Library
15616 East Highway 24
Independence, MO 64050

Credits

Editors
PeriSean Hall
www.theworddoctor44.com

Kim Bondafini
www.to-the-letter.com

Book & Website Designer
Sean Love
www.The-LoveGroup.com

Historian/Researcher
Mary M. White
Affiliated with New Orleans Public Library

Photography
Portraits:
Broderick Maxwell (Noted BM)
Tamaya Steen (Noted TS)

Devastation Photos: Alexey Sergeev — www.asergeev.com

Louisiana Division/City Archives
New Orleans Public Library

Copyright © 2010 Write Creations

All rights reserved. No part of this book may be reproduced without written permission from the author and publisher, except by a reviewer who may quote brief passages with appropriate credit; nor may any part of this book be reproduced, stored in a retrieval system, or transmitted in any form or by any electronic means, mechanical, photocopying, recording, or other, without written permission from the author and publisher.

ISBN: 978-0-9706292-1-0

Dedication
To my parents, Lynn Gray Norris and Albert Baron Norris,
All that I am or ever hope to be, I owe to you.

INTRODUCTION

WITHDRAW
from records of
Mid-Continent Public Library

My Story
Lynette Wilkinson

That's me. Standing in front of our home in the Lower Ninth Ward of New Orleans with my two brothers after church one Sunday. I was wearing a scratchy wool sweater I wanted off, but my mom insisted I wear it while we take a picture. I was not happy about the situation, and it shows!

I have so many memories of growing up in the Lower Ninth Ward that make my heart smile. For instance, Macarty School, that hands-down had the biggest and the best 5-cent vanilla cookies this kindergartner can remember. I also remember walking home with friends from McDonogh 19 Elementary carrying a heavy violin almost as big as I was, and walking past Fradella's Grocery, which sold the meat that made the best fried luncheon-meat sandwiches. I often think about singing our favorite R&B songs on the days we got a break from gym class at Lawless Junior High. Another fun memory was taking driver's ed at McDonogh 35, where one day the instructor/physical education teacher Mr. Phillips slammed on the brakes and exclaimed, "Girl, you do some stupid things!" There were also family holiday dinners when everybody, and I mean everybody, took a sip of Morgan David wine, only to later see my grandmother get up and dance a little jig being

full with the "spirit." Another fun thing we did was dress up for carnival and head uptown to my godmother's house to see the Mardi Gras parades. I'd spend summers at her house with her daughters and we'd go out in the backyard and get wet with the Water Wiggle hose as it chased us around the yard. Here's a series of other events we took part in: stopping by McKenzie's Bakery for some drop donuts … my mom taking me to Maison Blanche on Canal St. at Christmas time to see Mr. Bingle, a big puppet snow fairy with an ice cream cone for a hat and holly leaves for wings, dancing with his puppet friends in the huge display window … riding bikes with my friends on Sundays across Claiborne Avenue … playing hopscotch on the sidewalk between my house and Ms. Mary's house … buying frozen cups in the summer from Ms. Dabon across the street … the time my mom had to back down from the top of the Claiborne Bridge because the drawbridge got stuck … dinner at Dooky Chase restaurant … going with my mom to Iota Phi Lambda sorority meetings and joining her neighborhood club members in a game of Pokeno … going to 7 a.m. services at Amozion Baptist Church where the line of boys marching up for communion stretched from the front of the church to the back … hanging out with my friends who had big families and feeling like a family member, too … riding and singing in the car with my dad, who had the best sense of humor … visiting my great-grandmother in Lafitte Project and playing with a girl next door named Jeanette … going by my cousin's house to get my hair done … our German Shepherd Tiger who dragged his bowl up and down the driveway in protest to when we were tardy with his meals, and shared a few drops of beer my dad placed in his bowl as they both sat in our backyard … hearing the theme of "The Young and the Restless" on TV during school break while the cold air outside and the heat from the red beans my grandmother was boiling on the

stove frosted our glass patio door ... the time my mom got mad at my dad because he waited too late to get our Christmas tree, and their three children had to settle for presents stacked in three piles on the sofas ... the 10 to 15 dolls I slept with every night and their hard plastic hands poking me in the eyes and back ... I remember it all with lots of hugs and kisses, love and laughter. It seemed there was always something to laugh about.

Of course, there were also times that made my heart cry, like when we lost my oldest brother too soon. He was killed by a guy drag racing down Claiborne Avenue. I also remember when the wind and floods of Hurricane Betsy swept through New Orleans and left three feet of water in our house. The difference between Hurricane Betsy and Hurricane Katrina is that with Betsy, some areas like ours were flooded, but uptown where my grandmother lived was okay, so we were able to stay with her. The other difference was when we were able to return home after Hurricane Betsy to build more memories. After Katrina, that was not possible for my family.

In this book I introduce you to 16 people who, just as I did, shared some of the same memories about living in the Lower Ninth Ward of New Orleans, below the Industrial Canal. Most of the people you'll meet are people in my "circle of concern," including family, close friends, former classmates, and church members. I want you to know that there is more to the residents of the Lower Ninth Ward than what you saw during the news coverage of Hurricane Katrina. These were hardworking, family-oriented people, who owned their homes, had a sense of community, and were contributing members of society.

My name is Lynette Norris Wilkinson, and this is my New Orleans Ninth Ward.

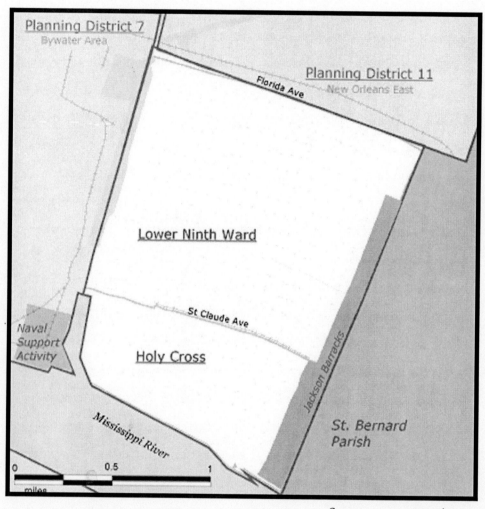

Source: www.gnocdc.org

The Beginning
Lower Ninth Ward

I was curious about the land where my family's home stood, so I asked New Orleans historian Mary White to do some research for me.

The area known as the Lower Ninth Ward, or the Lower 9 as it's called, is located less than five miles from the world-famous Bourbon Street. It began as a wooded area toppled with soil and was made fertile over time by the water that flowed from the Mississippi River. This land was known for producing crops of tobacco, rice, grains, and vegetables on the plantations. The plantations faced the river and were narrow but deep—access to the river for transportation purposes being the most important asset. These long, narrow parcels of land were usually two to four arpents wide and 40 to 80 arpents deep. Arpents were French units of measure that equaled about 192 feet. The land between the river and St. Claude Avenue was developed first, with St. Claude Avenue being at the 40 arpent line from the river, then later to Claiborne Avenue, which represented the 80 arpent line further away from the river.

The Lower Ninth Ward was created when boundary lines in New

Orleans were redrawn in 1852. The area consisted mostly of small farms and scattered houses. The city did not install proper drainage in the area until 1910 to 1920, although the project had been approved more than 10 years earlier. The lack of proper drainage and sewage, however, did not stop poor European immigrants and former slaves from flocking to the area to search for affordable housing, work in nearby industries, and live together in racial harmony. The wide-open spaces gave the area a rural feel, and the neighborly friendliness was appealing to its inhabitants. In 1923 the construction of the Industrial Canal further isolated the area from the rest of the city, dividing the Ninth Ward into the upper and lower sections. Thus, the Lower Ninth Ward referred not so much to the altitude of the land but more to its proximity to the mouth of the river below the Industrial Canal. The Lower 9 is bounded by the Industrial Canal to the west, the river to the south, the St. Bernard Parish to the east, and Florida Avenue to the north. It's about two miles from north to south. A subdivision of the Lower 9, the area known as Holy Cross, named for a popular school in the area, is located between St. Claude and the river. As time went on, homes were built. After World War II, large grocery chains took over the marketing of produce and the chains became centered, for the most part, in California. Small growers were forced out of business and, as a result, the land became ripe for residential development. Still, by 1950, only half of the Lower 9 was developed. It was during the 1950's that most of the home construction occurred.

The route along St. Claude became dotted with corner groceries and retail stores. Commercial activity and home development were still growing in 1965 when Hurricane Betsy struck. Hurricane Betsy drowned the Lower

9—80 percent of the area was underwater and 81 people lost their lives in the storm. The eight-foot levee was just no match for Betsy's 10-foot storm surge. People walked through waist-high water and waited on roofs to be rescued. Some say the lack of financial assistance following Hurricane Betsy prohibited the revitalization of the area, forcing many businesses and longtime residents to move out. This signaled the beginning of a decline in the neighborhood. Still, these working-class residents kept their strong ties to faith, family, and community.

Reacting to what seemed like neglect from city officials, residents of the Lower 9 formed their own civic groups to help secure needed community services and funding for the area. The community activism caught the eye of the school desegregation movement, and in 1960 the all-white McDonogh #19 School on St. Claude Avenue in the Lower 9 became one of the first schools in the Orleans Parish School Board System to open its doors to black children since the Reconstruction. The event was marked by widespread media attention and angry protests. After the desegregation of McDonogh #19, whites began a mass exodus to nearby St. Bernard Parish.

One of the well-known community hubs of the Lower 9 was the Andrew P. Sanchez Sr. Multi-Service Center located at Claiborne Avenue and Caffin Avenue. The center housed several community services, including a health clinic, the Head Start program, a police substation, and an adjoining senior citizen center. Across the street was the Martin Luther King Elementary School (formerly Macarty School), which housed the Lower Ninth Ward's first full-service library.

In addition to being home to some 15,000 residents, 60 percent of which

were homeowners, the Lower Ninth Ward, more than any other part of the city, was home to many small businesses such as corner stores, Laundromats, beauty shops, barbers, and many churches. Several famous people came from the Lower Ninth Ward, including rock-and-roll legend Fats Domino; renowned band leader, vocalist, and trumpeter Kermit Ruffin; and poet Kalamu ya Salaam.

The land where my family's home stood was once part of a plantation owned by Dr. William Flood. Upon his passing, his land was subsequently divided into lots by his executor in 1824. (Flood Street in the Lower Ninth Ward was named after him). However, records documenting the right to concession made by the French government show the property existed as early as 1758.

According to property records, the land that was formerly Dr. Flood's was acquired at a public sale by the firm of Hunter, Murphy and Talbott and sold to August Ferrier Jr. in March 1852. Ferrier sold the property to Stoddard Howell in 1859, and Howell sold to Mrs. Victorine Cabos in 1888. When Mrs. Cabos died her children, Paul H. Laguens and Marie Pauline Laguens, divided the property in August 1918. Marie took possession of the square of ground where my family's home stood. When Marie passed her daughter, Mrs. Marie LePoutge, inherited the property in January 1932. Marie LePoutge and her husband, Leon Sarrat, sold the property to Eugene T. Calongne in November 1936. A side note: Research shows a Eugene T. Calongne as an area movie producer who, along with Jules Sevin, produced the feature motion picture, "The Wacky World of Dr. Morgus." The movie was based on the early 1960s TV horror-movie host, Doctor Morgus (aka "Morgus the Magnificent" and "Momis Alexander Morgus").

In January 1950, Mrs. Melba Ann Calongne Sevin and Eugene T. Calongne Jr. sold the property to Neil Christopher and Hans Schlesinger. Just a few months later, Christopher and Schlesinger sold a lot on that square to my parents, Albert and Lynn Norris, on April 5, 1950.

My two brothers and I grew up in that house. It remained our family home until August 2005, when Hurricane Katrina unleashed its fury with a vengeance, leaving the home as a hollow shell inhabited by the ghosts of memories.

And the rest, as they say, is history.

Stories of Survival, Faith, and Hope

Denise

"After I heard the news of the flooding, I went to my mother's room and knocked on the door. She opened the door and just stood there. Then she sat on the bed, no tears pouring from her eyes, just a glossy look. I think she felt—lost."

When my family and I heard Hurricane Katrina was coming I thought, 'Here we go again.' Only a few months ago, we were caught in gridlock for hours trying to escape Hurricane Ivan. This time I said I was staying put and not going. My mother would not have been happy with that decision however, and I knew she would have been concerned about me, so I left.

My family and I left Sunday about 10:30 a.m. I had already made reservations at a hotel in Bossier City, just outside of Shreveport, figuring we'd be there Sunday and Monday. Before we left New Orleans, we picked up everything off the floor. The house was four feet off the ground and when Hurricane Betsy struck, we only had three feet of water so we figured we might get a foot of water at the most. It was close to the beginning of school, so I brought a tote bag with the kids' school records, birth certificates, and report cards. I also took clothes for a couple of days.

11

Roads were packed with cars in every condition, from good to not good at all. We were on a trip that should have taken six hours, but by 3 p.m. we were still several hours away. I saw people running out of gas and going to the woods to use the restroom. The gas attendants had evacuated and you couldn't use cash at the pumps, so unless you had a credit card you were out of luck. We all loaned the use of our credit cards for cash so we could get back on the road. This involved assisting people we did not know.

Our 15-passenger Dodge van was packed to the hills with people, things, and two small puppies. As we drove, the wind began to rock the van. We could see the clouds circling above in the sky. We had older people and children in the car, so we had to get to a safe place quickly. We arrived at the hotel at approximately 7:30 p.m.

I woke up Monday at 7:30 a.m. to the news on TV that the Ninth Ward was under water. I felt exasperated. All I saw was water and tiny trees, and from the landscape I knew it was New Orleans East by the lake. Ironically, the news showed the "Flood St." sign in the Ninth Ward, and that's all that could be seen. The water level was that high. As the news cameras panned backward, all that could be seen was the vastness of water. This is what I woke up to on Monday morning. I wondered if my mom was asleep and if she saw this.

Tears filled the kids' eyes and I just sat there. I thought it can't be happening. We're supposed to go back. This was supposed to be like a vacation. The kids get out of school, we visit our friends like we did during Hurricane Ivan, and we turn around and go back. It was supposed to be a vacation.

I went to my mother's room and knocked on the door. She opened the door and just stood there. Then she sat on the bed, no tears pouring from her eyes, just a glossy look. I think she felt—lost. It's like losing parents, like an

orphan. That's exactly how it felt.

I know she felt lost because everything was in the house—pictures of my grandmother, pictures of us as kids, my grandmother's sewing machine, my grandmother's picture from when she was a nurse, my grandfather's picture, post office employment pins, and military service medals of my brothers—a lot of memories. The top of my wedding cake was in the dining room china cabinet. I lost my kids' baby pictures, an academic and athletic awards—all that was in there. We even lost Esther. Esther was a little turtle we got for my oldest daughter when she was in the 6th grade. I home schooled my daughter, and we got Esther at a science field trip she took with a close school friend. Esther was huge and she knew us. We took Esther with us when we evacuated for Hurricane Ivan, but we left her during Katrina. We found Esther's shell in the rubble under the house. My daughter cried and sobbed so hard like a baby; she was a junior in college, but I knew losing Esther hurt her deeply. The first time we came back to New Orleans after Hurricane Katrina, as we approached the Kenner line, we could smell the stench, the smell of decay and death. The area was very still. There were not a lot of people around. Devastation was everywhere, especially in the Ninth Ward. The smells were stronger there and overwhelming. It looked like someone had dropped a bomb. I was not prepared for this.

As we went slipping and sliding through the sludge to get to our house, we could see that solid wood had crumbled like mush. Inside I noticed that my bedroom dresser had disintegrated. How could the refrigerator get from the kitchen to the dining room? Yet, there was a picture of Jesus on the wall of Mom's bedroom still in place. It never came off the wall. Unbelievable! All the other pictures were off the wall, but that one remained. There was mold and mildew and maggots everywhere, but nothing on that picture. I believe

with all my heart that picture was there to remind us we have a hope.

There's a flavor to New Orleans that you just won't find anywhere else. It's not just the food, it's the people. Before Katrina, I had a lot of family, friends, and church family. We participated in community events. I grew up in a neighborhood where everybody knew everybody. Even if you were in another part of town, someone would say, "Hey, I know you." If they didn't know you, they knew your people or someone in your family. It was no big deal to strike up a conversation. Our family was close—a big extended family of aunts and uncles and cousins. We were always together. Because my grandmother's house was large, we always had family gatherings there. My life was filled with a lot of constant activity.

We had a corner grocery store (not everybody has a corner grocery store), and it sold all kinds of staples and candy. I remember my cousins and me taking 25 cents each, then we each would get two-for-a-penny candies and cookies and a Big Shot soft drink for our penny party. I remember Christmas parties and yard parties with hamburgers, walking two blocks to St. Claude to Puglias Supermarket and walking several blocks to school. I remember having fun with my lifelong school friends.

At the time of Katrina I had a daughter in kindergarten, a daughter in 7th grade, a son who had graduated from high school and had just started college, and a daughter in her junior year in college studying to become an athletic trainer. My oldest daughter lost all her clothes during Katrina, so as the fall and winter months approached, she had to walk around her college campus in her uniform shorts for her clinicals because she had no money to buy the long khaki pants required. She was told she could not receive assistance when she contacted Louisiana Health and Human Services because she didn't have any children; she was not a single or unwed mother. Go

figure! She lost everything in Katrina and she was dislocated, yet she still pressed on to complete her degree and become a contributor in society, but she does not qualify? My son had just arrived at college and communication was a big problem. At first, I didn't know where he was. We dropped him off at the campus the Thursday before the hurricane. The university was not expecting to have a major disruption in their school schedule, yet the land and cell lines were down. I did not know whether he was really safe on campus. I didn't see or hear from him for three weeks. Then, out of nowhere there was a temporary opening in cell communication and he called my cell. I called out to those around, "It's Micah." He said that all he wanted for his birthday was to see his family. Then, Hurricane Rita came on the scene and the university closed. He was able to travel with an Impact Ministries friend and his family to Shreveport, and we met him there and drove back to Dallas on his 18th birthday.

As devastating as Katrina was, and as much as people tried to grasp what had taken place, getting assistance to get back on our feet was very challenging. So many people needed help. Everybody in New Orleans was going through the same thing so who were you going to go to for help? The government seemingly had no clue. I didn't receive any assistance until the end of November. If you were not on welfare, like we weren't, it seemed like assistance was not readily available. It was also frustrating having to settle with property insurers.

We had to deal with being called refugees. We were not coming from another country. We were born and raised in the United States. We are people who were educated, raised their children in the school system and universities, and needed to be treated with honor and dignity. We were considered transient because we were uprooted, but we didn't choose to

move. One key thing to know is that a lot of people in the Lower Ninth Ward owned their home. The way they were portrayed in news coverage undermined people, as if they had no roots. Yes, you may have seen the people toting things, but they may not have had a way to leave and so they just stayed. Don't assume everybody is the same. The people were poor and from various other economic and social backgrounds all mixed in together. People say, "Just get over it." We say, "We can't just get over it because our individual lives, our academic lives, and our family lives were changed. We lost everything. We lost *everything*. We had to take time to regroup. It's like having a 1,000-piece puzzle and some pieces are missing. You're trying to get it to look like the picture on the puzzle box. You're trying to figure out how to reestablish consistency in your relationships with your family while still dealing with health issues, the loss of jobs, and other life conditions that everyone else deals with from time to time. I say until it happens to you, you can't understand.

More than anything, I wanted some sense of normalcy for my children. They had been taken away from family and friends, and our family is now scattered across Mississippi, Oklahoma, and Louisiana. Life became fragmented. We were used to sisters and brothers and everybody getting together for birthdays and all other life events. Now I can count on one hand how many times I have seen my son. The distance makes it worse.

Our neighborhood in New Orleans is divided. Some areas are rebuilding faster than others. Several homes on our street have been renovated, though. The best way to describe my life now is I'm just getting some normalcy. I'm caught between a rock and a hard place. I wanted to be home, but it's not the same in New Orleans. Dallas is home now. I live here, I attend church here, and my kids attend school here, but there are no roots. It's good for my

kids to be here for the school system, but I've had a difficult time finding a full-time job as an administrative assistant. I want to be rooted and grounded again. I'm still adjusting and I'm blessed to have my faith and a good support system. Still, it's different. I can't say I know Dallas like I know New Orleans and New Orleans knows me.

Micah

"I miss the culture, and the fact that you could always find somewhere to play basketball."

My life before Katrina consisted of playing baseball in high school, working in the afternoons after school, and doing the normal things a guy would do to transition and prepare for college. When Katrina hit, I had only been in college in Lafayette, Louisiana, for a couple of days. I only had a couple of week's clothing with me. Everything else I left at home in the Lower Ninth Ward because I was expecting to go back to visit for Labor Day and get everything else. I lost just about everything in Katrina.

One thing about the Ninth Ward was you could stop and grab something to eat at a corner grocery. There was one on just about every corner. I miss the culture, and the fact that you could always find somewhere to play basketball. You just don't find that everywhere—only in New Orleans. I really miss being able to go out to the lake front to hang out or just chill. My mom and I used to go there all the time. The lake front route that travels west toward Canal Boulevard is shut down on weekends, and this makes it easy to find parking.

I was separated from my family when Katrina hit, and when it happened I did what I knew to do and that was to pray for my family. I rode out the storm at my school. My adult counselors helped me a lot because I could talk to them about what I was going through. I wasn't able to get in contact with my family for three weeks, and when I did it was done via text and through the use of someone else's phone. I didn't see my family until I went to visit them in Dallas for my 18th birthday in September. At that time my university was closed for the expected arrival of Hurricane Rita.

I know there were a lot of challenges for my family following Katrina: finding a house, finding a job, figuring out how to pay bills, getting my sisters in school … the standard stuff you go through when you move, except you have lost everything.

I didn't see the house in the Lower Ninth Ward until the following spring because I had to study and couldn't leave school. When I saw it, I was surprised and frustrated over the levee. I had studied in school about the redesign of the levee, realizing it would take $10 to 15 million to rebuild. Now, it will take billions to rebuild the area. A lot of people feel the government and politicians should have never let this happen again. They had hundreds of buses in the parking lot. They could have saved the buses and the people. You have to realize that people stayed because there was no way to leave.

I miss having the photos from all the trips I had taken in high school. I had taken a lot of trips, like a trip to Nevada, and some of the pictures were never even developed. I lost my cap and gown, my baseball uniforms, and other memorabilia from high school that I can never replace.

Even with all we lost, maybe it was easier for us because there was no loss of life. Everyone survived. When lives are lost and property is lost, it is even more devastating.

I graduated from college last spring with a degree in environmental science. I took time during the summer to work in Montgomery with an urban ministry to offer support to young boys with or without fathers. In the fall I intend to begin employment in the field of coastal restoration, either in an educational role or mini projects in the field. I plan to live in Lafayette, Louisiana.

When hurricanes approach now, I don't feel fear. I understand now that the best way to prevention is to be prepared. I just pray for the best. After all, what's the worst that could happen? It already did.

Photo by Alexey Sergeev

Stanley & Betty

"Our house sits in front of a wide-open field with nothing to restrict the flow of the water. We watched in shock as water rushed across the field, some waves soaring at least 25 feet in the air. We had 14 ½ feet of water in our house in 10 minutes. It was just a horrible sight to see."

STANLEY ...

My parents migrated out of St. Bernard Parish, which is an outer parish a few miles from the Lower Ninth Ward. We've always owned our own home. We lived in the first house until 1965 when we were hit with Hurricane Betsy. My journey began in the Lower Ninth Ward. I guess you could say I was born and raised there.

Katrina is actually the second major storm I've survived. You may remember Hurricane Betsy, which happened when I was in the 4th grade. During Betsy, a lot of people were able to go to the uptown area of New Orleans because they had relatives who lived there and that area wasn't affected that badly. We had relatives living in the Magnolia Housing Projects so that's where we went. That experience made me reflect upon the fact that

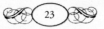

you don't ever want to get to where you don't know where you're going to lay your head. We had to live in the Magnolia Projects for two or two and a half months until we were able to return to our home in the Lower Ninth Ward. I started out working as an auto mechanic before moving on to become a master diesel mechanic. Then I went to Delgado Community College to study body and fender technology, and from there I went on to own my own custom automotive restoration shop. So that's actually what I do; I restore cars. I'm still doing that to this day. My wife and I met while in high school. She transferred to McDonogh #35 after our sophomore year. We have been married for 35 years; we married right out of high school. I graduated from George Washington Carver Senior High and my wife graduated from McDonogh #35. I attended Carver because it offered the auto mechanics program I was so interested in. My class from junior high school, Alfred Lawless Junior High, was the only class that did not have a graduation exercise. The reason we did not have a graduation ceremony was because of a fight that broke out in the cafeteria. It just so happened we had some dignitaries visiting the school that day. The principal was so mad he cancelled our graduation. Later on that day one of our classmates threw a party for us. We had a big party uptown, but we didn't get a graduation. They just gave us our diplomas and sent us on our way. We had an outstanding class, though; some very intelligent students came out of that class. Doctors, lawyers, architects, small-business men and women, and teachers.

Before Hurricane Katrina hit, we were at home, trying to pay tuition, and buy school supplies, uniforms, etc., to send and educate our daughters in all these private schools. I have four daughters and I'm raising two nieces, who are my wife's brother's two daughters. At the time of Katrina, our oldest daughter was already in her own home, had graduated from college, and was

working and self-supporting. She had recently purchased her own house in the Gentilly area. I only have two of my daughters and my two nieces still at home now. One niece is at Xavier Prep and the others are at St. Stephen's Central School.

Growing up, I really loved playing basketball at all the parks. Back there by Lawless school, you could stop your car at any given moment and come out with a basketball and have a pickup game on the spot. You know, it was just a thrill to be able to ride around the Lower Ninth Ward and go down just about any street or any corner and wave at neighbors and friends that you knew. Or you might have a party or something in the backyard, or just walk home from school and sit on the porch. So it was just a place, you know, a community that you grew up in—very close-knit, where you knew everybody. I have so many good memories.

Katrina really caught us at a time when we were at an all-time low on finances. School had just started and we had just paid all the kids' tuition, so we really didn't have the kind of finances to go somewhere else and sustain ourselves for a long period of time. I think that was one of the problems a lot of people faced; it was so close to the end of the month, you know, when people are waiting on their next paycheck or allotment of money to come in. They were now faced with making this departure from New Orleans and then having to sustain themselves for who knew how long. You also have to remember that many did not evacuate because they had evacuated not too long ago because of Hurricane Ivan. It was a very long road trip, and the storm did not even come our way. Many thought it would be the same way this time. How would you do it without finances? So we basically did what we would do when these storm threats came: We went to the second floor of our home where it was safe. Our house is pretty high up and made of brick

and we had a generator up there and a small ice box. We decided that we would just go upstairs and pray and ask God to not to let anything too bad happen. Unfortunately, no one could have expected the magnitude of this one, but thank God that due to the fact this house was built with an upstairs, God prepared us like He prepared Noah with the ark. We were just blessed to be up there and able to ride that storm out because it was devastating. We had 15 people in that house—men, women, and kids.

Our house sits in front of a wide-open field with nothing to restrict the flow of the water. We watched in shock as water rushed across the field, some waves soaring at least 25 feet in the air. We had 14½ feet of water in our house in 10 minutes. It was just a horrible sight to see.

We were actually able to ride out the entire storm in that house. We were rescued a few days later when workers from the Louisiana Wildlife and Fisheries came by with the fire department. One of my good friends from the Lower Ninth Ward was one of the firemen. He is the husband of one of the former teachers from St. David School where my wife, her siblings, and all of my children received their elementary education. Talk about a small world, right? We were able to come right out to the second story balcony and climb right down into the boat. From there, we departed down to Poland Avenue. Thank God we didn't have any loss of life.

My family and I were separated at the Poland Avenue area. I was born with polio and I really couldn't walk that far. I told them to go on. News that the levee might have another breach frightened them, so they went on. I crossed to the other side of the river and was picked up and taken to the convention center. I didn't really get connected with them again until two and a half weeks later when I found out they were way in Shreveport. It was kind of hard, you know, not knowing where my family was.

I stayed down there at the convention center for three days with no food and water or other items needed for daily health care. Finally the buses arrived to transport us. The situation was tough; there were a lot of senior citizens with no one to help them. So I gathered maybe seven guys that I grew up with in the neighborhood through the years and told them to stay behind and try to give the National Guard a hand. It would have been inhumane of us to board the buses ahead of the senior citizens, so we stayed back and helped the National Guard until all the senior citizens boarded the buses, and then we boarded a bus. It was the last bus leaving the convention center.

We thought that the bus was taking us to Atlanta, but they had accepted all the evacuees that they could so the bus we were on took us to Alabama. The National Guard really thanked us because, like I said, they really needed a hand. I just thank God for doing that deed. From that point on, I can tell you it really has been a blessing.

My family and I stayed in Birmingham, Alabama, almost a year. A guy there had a vacant home and actually invited us to live in the house rent-free. It needed a little repairing, which a group of volunteers and I were able to do, and they helped me get it ready for me and my family. I then was able to quickly go to work and was able to save enough money to purchase the house up there. Now we actually have a place to go if another storm comes. Remember, I learned long ago to never be in a situation where you don't know where you are going to lay your head. In fact, we just recently went back to our house in Birmingham when hurricanes Gustav and Ike came. Praise God we had the house. Otherwise, we would have been in a shelter like everyone else.

People really treated us wonderfully in Alabama. My wife returned to New Orleans first and went back to work, and the kids went back to school.

One of my daughters graduated from the MAX. The MAX School was created as a result of Hurricane Katrina. It was the combination of St. Mary's Academy students, St. Augustine students, Xavier University Preparatory Senior High School students, a few students from other Catholic high schools, and a few public schools. This was really necessary since 80 percent of the city had sustained damage from the hurricane. Hurricane Katrina had damaged the campuses of St. Mary's and St. Augustine, but Prep's campus was virtually unscathed. The MAX graduation was a ceremony of the seniors from St. Mary's, St. Augustine, and Xavier Prep schools combined. Those schools had their own graduations, so our students actually graduated twice from high school in the same year.

After I came back to New Orleans, my wife's supervisor who works with one of the social justice ministries (both before and after Hurricane Katrina) passed by one day and told me she had some wonderful students here to help New Orleans residents but they didn't have enough work for them to do. So she told me if I needed any help to let her know. And that's how I met some wonderful students from the University of Central Florida. My house was in the cleaning and gutting process, so I told her to bring them by. Three of them came (two guys and a lady) and they just jumped in and did whatever needed to be done. I just tried to encourage them and let them know that God will truly bless them for taking time out of their busy schedules to help. They said they were just here to help whoever needed it. I told them what a great deed it was and that I truly appreciated what they were doing. The next morning they came back and there were 30 of them. Dr. Richard Lapchick, one of the directors of the sports management division of the school, was also there and was really a wonderful guy. The students were so inspired by me talking to them that they went back to the university and opened a

foundation in my name called Hope for Stanley. Little did we know that one of the guys that was with them heard our story and was so moved that he went back home to Massachusetts and gathered a group of businessmen and craftsmen. He also gathered all the goods and items needed to refurbish a home and joined forces with Dr. Lapchick to make things happen. This great partnership, coupled with funds generated from the foundation, refurbished our home. These students made several trips to help us paint, plant, and make our house a home again. The students continue to make several trips here out of their concern to help the rebuilding process for the citizens of New Orleans. They've been back and forth working to refurbish parks, homes, churches, etc. They have really made a difference in the 16 trips over a couple of years they have made to New Orleans. In fact, it is part of the curriculum for the students to come down for a week of community service. My home is like the headquarters so whenever they come, there may be a group of about 60 or more volunteers. We just cook and barbecue and do whatever we can to make them feel comfortable while they are here. A lot of these students use their own money to get here.

Looking at the progress and infrastructure of the city, it is a shame to see that the Lower Ninth Ward is still in a very devastated condition. That's very hard to see. Going toward Florida Avenue across Claiborne Avenue, you can clearly see that the area is having a difficult time trying to recover. The land where Lawless school once stood is cleared and there's nothing standing. And when you look at that history and the monuments that once stood, they are all gone; it's really devastating. All in all, it's still a long path until the Lower Ninth Ward is really back in working condition because the struggle continues.

BETTY ...

Surprisingly we are doing well in spite of it all. As I look back, it is an amazing journey we have endured. It is still really hard to digest, all the devastation, loss of life, homes, mementoes, etc. Looking at the big picture, there is still a whole lot to be done even though we seem to have made so much progress. It's a blessing to reach my age and this time of my life and still get through the Katrina process. I look at so many people who did not make it or lost their lives during the rebuilding process. This is really beyond all my imagination and dreams. I thank God for not allowing it to be more than what it was. A lot of people who haven't lived or been exposed to the total devastation we experienced don't understand. Every time we look around there's something we miss or we don't have anymore because of Katrina. There were certain relics my grandmother had given me such as a birthstone ring and a Bible, and those are things that can't be replaced. Our whole world has changed. Sometimes, I still look for the rosaries I received as a gift from my great-grandmother; or perhaps in other cases, a network or support system of friends and relatives, all of which are now gone. That was the hardest thing for me. I'm grateful we didn't lose anybody, but now everybody is scattered from California to New Mexico. It's just going to take time. We'll have to start making new memories.

After all the city has been through, there is still a racial divide. After Katrina there were not that many churches open. My church was clustered, meaning we held joint services with another Catholic church, a church with Caucasian members. The first service was absolutely wonderful. I thought that people had really changed. We were able to worship in unison, all together worshipping one God. At the first service, there were 150 Caucasians and about 75 African Americans. At the next service, there were about 100

African Americans and about 75 Caucasians. At the next services, there were more and more of our members than the others. Finally, after about a month or so of services, only three people from the Caucasian church showed up in comparison to the hundreds of parishioners from our church. We realized later that a meeting was held and it was said that their parishioners from the Caucasian church would not return as long as those people are there. Their church is a large brick and mortar facility with high ceilings and marble floors; our congregation could not afford to rebuild this building nor could we afford the heating and cooling costs. So after our assessment and the people's input, we were allowed to return to our church on St. Claude Avenue. Believe it or not, this is ridiculous. After all we've been through and all they've been through, why can't we sit in the same church? Other people from all over the country can come down and helped us get back on our feet and we can't even worship together? When we were in 6th grade, we never thought we'd see an African American president. We had an exercise in school to predict when an African American would be elected to the Oval Office and most of us said we did not think we would ever see it. How wrong were we? I actually got a chance to meet President Obama when he visited the Gentilly area of New Orleans. He even worked with Habitat for Humanity. I said to myself, "This is an anointed man. He's very calm. He will listen to advice." I pray for him every day.

We lived in four different cities before we came back to New Orleans. Everybody wanted to know why we wanted to come back to a crime-ridden city. Everywhere we went we had to defend our city. Many people go by what they see on television. We know that what you see on TV is not indicative of everybody in New Orleans. The media accentuates the negative. There are many young people obtaining good grades and doing a

lot of positive things that never make the news. When we have Career Day and our African American dignitaries and business people come to make presentations to our students, the media doesn't even show up, despite the fact that we invited them. But good things happen; history happens every day. Everybody has a story to tell, and it's not always negative. Every New Orleanian has a Katrina Story.

The majority of deaths that occurred during Katrina were due to of a lack of resources. Many people did not have the money needed to leave the city. Many were not as prepared as they should have been. But even if you were, the closer you were to the levee breach, the less likely the odds of surviving. Many people likened their experience to the "fear factor." They had to climb trees, and swing from tree to tree to get to a point of safety. Others used refrigerator doors as a makeshift boat and paddled their way to a nearby levee, or the bridge, or somewhere dry. This storm hit with a vengeance. It was more powerful than Hurricane Betsy. I am a Hurricane Betsy survivor. It angered me when people called us evacuees. We were born, raised, and paid our taxes in this city. We are survivors, not evacuees. How can you be an evacuee when you helped to make your city prosper? As I look back, even though I was in elementary school and the age of my youngest daughter, I remember Hurricane Betsy. When Hurricane Betsy hit, the Red Cross was here. They were in the shelters and they set them up with food, water, and staples to sustain life. They utilized resources and other outlets to help family members locate their missing relatives. I expected the same with Hurricane Katrina. What a difference it was with Katrina. We felt like we had to do everything we could to survive. It was a hard thing to go through. It was a matter of survival. People did what they needed to do to survive. We were left to fend for ourselves. We went into stores to get food and cooked right

out on the street. Men looked out for women and children. They got drinks, meat, and bread so people would not perish.

After the first year of the rebuild, the French Quarter was shown in the media to be back up and running. To the eyes of a tourist things were back to normal, but not to the native New Orleanian. We could see it was only up about 50 percent, not the 100 percent the media portrayed. And the city was less than 25 percent back in operation at that time because if you went into the areas where the residents lived, you would have seen that it was far from all right. I had never seen my city in such a poor state. In fact, when we came home for Christmas after Katrina, the earth was still crunching under my feet. Trees were brown and there were no birds singing. Every block had maybe one or two residents who had moved back. Many people didn't even have a trailer. A lot of people didn't want to come back because they didn't know who their neighbors would be or if they would even have a neighbor. Nothing is in walking distance. Now, the only thing you really have in the neighborhood is a gas station and a Laundromat. There are not enough services. We do not have anything in place to provide even the basic services. We have one school, and it's not big enough to house kindergarten to 12th grade. This was at one time an area that had four elementary schools and one high school. That is not counting the four private schools. People who have children have a very tough choice to make. If you take away all the educational institutions, what is left in the community? We don't have any parks, stores, medical facilities, grocery stores, or even a pharmacy. There is a lot of busing as well. Little kids get shuffled around. It's just outrageous!

I'm not saying we're not hopeful, but we do have to hold our politicians accountable. We must hold onto knowing that when we mobilize and return, the people can make a difference. We have to do it for those who are

not here. We have to stand up and become the voice of those who cannot return, especially our seniors who cannot return due to a lack of services and resources. This whole experience was a lot more than what we bargained for and we just have to pray that things will get better.

I just have too much at stake to give up. God will never leave us or forsake us. We know He is with us every step of the way. It has been our faith, faith-based organizations, and all the wonderful volunteers that have given us the encouragement we needed to continue. I had to come back to New Orleans. I had one daughter graduating from high school. She poured so much into her high school years that I had to make sure that she would participate in the culmination of these important years of her life, including being there for her high school graduation. And then my little one, she was also suffering. It was really hard for her to readjust to a different school, to lose all of her friends and her home, and become isolated from her family all at one time. For some strange reason she felt responsible. In some cities, people made our kids feel inferior, so I had to go to bat for my kids. It wasn't that their education in New Orleans was inferior; they just needed an opportunity to use their skills. The subjects were just presented differently and as a result, sometimes they had difficulty adjusting to the new presentations. When given a chance, they excel and will continue to excel beyond expectations. I told teachers, "You just have to give them a chance." A lot of parents didn't do that for their children and they allowed school administrators to put the children in certain classes like a special New Orleans class or label them as slow. Sometimes administrators did it under the guise of giving students grieving space or providing them with emotional support by separating and isolating them from the student body. I hated for that to happen, so I promised my kids when the schools opened again in New

Orleans, that's where we were going.

Right now, we're just trying to piece things together and get comfortable. So far everybody's doing okay, so that's a blessing. We have lost a lot of people though, even those who were not really sick. I believe that grief, stress, and the inability to put their lives back together quickly killed a lot of people. At one point I was going to a funeral a week, sometimes two per week. I got to the point that I just could not go to another funeral.

While we were in the "diaspora" as they put it, I thought of everything I missed. I missed the "good mornings" wished to me each morning by a perfect stranger. I missed all the little ones from my daughters' elementary school who came to give me a hug or a good morning wish. I missed the daily greetings of the teachers, cafeteria manager, and staff who asked me, "How ya doin'?" or "Howze ya momma n nem'?" These famous New Orleans greetings that only New Orleanians give are the things we have come to appreciate and miss so dearly. I miss our church, the familiar hymns, and clapping or standing up and swaying with a hymn that touches my soul. I really love my city. I love the people because it is really the people that make the city and not the city that makes the people. I still say that New Orleans is the biggest, smallest place in the world. We love it, and now that the Saints are marching in and have become the World Champions, "Who Dat? We Dat, We all that plus! We love Dat, We're the Champions." Finally, and at last! God Bless everyone. We can do whatever our heart's desire. The sky is really the limit.

Photo by Alexey Sergeev

Juliet

"I miss the way the neighborhood was before Katrina. There was always somebody outside who could tell you what was going on. We had a lot of togetherness and everybody knew everybody."

We left New Orleans escaping Hurricane Katrina heading to Baton Rouge, but Baton Rouge was packed so we kept on going to Alexandria, Louisiana. I heard some of the elderly passed away on the highway because they were on the road for so long and became dehydrated. It was so sad. My family and I ended up at a relative's house in Alexandria. We stayed in Alexandria two years. I waited for the school system in New Orleans to pull things together before I returned with my kids.

My life before Katrina was wonderful. In addition to being a photographer, I was a math teacher at Carver High School. I coached the girl's volleyball team and also helped with the girl's basketball team. The basketball team made it to the state play-offs for the first time when I was there. When we took the trip to state, that was the first time some of the girls had even been to Baton Rouge.

My kids and I spent the weekends playing ball or going to the movies. That's one thing we missed when we were in Alexandria. It was very quiet and low-key there and there wasn't much for my kids to do. They were used to being active.

I miss the way the neighborhood was before Katrina. There was always somebody outside who could tell you what was going on. We had a lot of togetherness and everybody knew everybody. If you did something bad on another street in the neighborhood, your mom would find out. One of my favorite memories is playing on the yard at St. David's Church.

We expected a little rain and a little flooding with Katrina, but nothing like what actually happened. When we left, we just packed enough clothes for the weekend. We had left the city many times before for hurricanes. This is what we do. We always leave and come back and everything is fine. This time we lost everything except for the clothes on our backs and some pictures we found, which we later were able to restore.

We knew some of the people who didn't survive. One man wouldn't leave. He wanted to stay and drink and party. His family found him on the sofa. Another escaped the hurricane and fled to California, only to be shot by another guy after he arrived.

The first time we saw our house after the flood was on an Internet site where somebody had posted pictures. The water was up to the top of the house and all we could see was the tip of the house. My mom looked at the picture and asked where the house was. We told her, "That's it." The first time I saw our house after Katrina, I wanted to cry.

After the hurricane, we had to battle with insurance companies over who was paying for the damage. One insurance company would say the damage was caused by water not wind. The other would say it's caused by wind not

water. Then, when we received payment and assistance, we were told we had been overpaid and were asked to send it back.

I miss family Sundays when everybody would go to church and then come to the house for Sunday dinner. Right now I am attending school to learn medical coding and billing. I don't know, I may eventually return to teaching one day.

New Orleans has new people now, but they're nice people. The city is coming back, slowly but surely. If it were not for the college kids from New York and California who volunteered to help us clean up and get back on our feet, especially the senior citizens, I don't know what we would have done.

One thing is for sure, though: Whenever the hurricanes come again, I'm leaving.

Photo by Alexey Sergeev

"Doochie"

"As we walked across the bridge, I saw Fats Domino, legendary New Orleans musician, who lived not too far from our house. I told him everything was flooded. He said, "Everything?" I said, "Everything. We've got 20 feet of water." He said, "Even my house?" I said, "Even your house." That's when he started singing one of his famous songs, "Ain't That A Shame."

The news announced that the hurricane was headed to New Orleans, and people were told to prepare to evacuate because newscasters didn't know the strength of the hurricane. If you couldn't leave, it was suggested that you stay in your attic. This was a really bad suggestion, because once you got in the attic you had to also have an escape from the attic through the roof as the waters rose.

The city shut down and stores and gas stations closed, so a lot of people, like in my situation, had access to a car but didn't have any gasoline in it. I knew some stores that stayed open and were determined to stay open as long as people were coming in, so I spent most of the day the Saturday before the storm helping people who were either trying to get out or stay.

By Sunday morning, people were faced with the realization that if they couldn't get out, they had to stay. I spent a lot of time bringing people in the neighborhood to the one store that I knew was open while I stayed in contact with my mother (via phone), as she and I were living together. I also called my children. I had decided I was going to ride out the storm, but I told my youngest daughter when they left to go to the Superdome for shelter, "Don't leave my mama." Thank God for my youngest daughter, Ashley. She got my mother out of that house. When I arrived home Sunday evening and saw my mother was gone, I knew then that my daughter had done what I asked her to do. She later told me that my mother was determined not to leave without hearing from me, so they had to tell her they were going to meet me at the Superdome. She had to lie to get my mother out, but God bless her for that. Once I got back home, it was just a matter of trying to prepare the house for the storm. The lights and phone went out. The wind and rain were steadily coming down as I tried to finish putting up the panels on the sliding glass patio door. I also covered the back door on the side of the house, which was solid wood and half glass. Once I did that, from the time I helped one last family, it would be 24 hours before I saw another living person.

I went in the house and changed clothes because I was soaking wet. There were about four or five inches of water on the ground from the constant rain, but it didn't seem like it was going to be a dangerous situation. I finished stacking and picking up everything off the floor out of reach from the water. I moved through the house with candles since the lights were out. I hadn't eaten anything, so I took some food out of the refrigerator and fixed something to eat. It was close to midnight. The wind and rain were still going on, beating against the house. When I finished eating I dozed off because I was exhausted.

I woke up at the break of dawn. It was very, very quiet. There was no

more rain or nothing. I thought it must be over. So I opened up the front door and it was like daybreak—quiet, and it was beautiful outside. I was thankful the storm was over. I began praying to God for everyone who went through the storm, and I thanked God for my mother, my daughters, my son and his family, and I prayed everybody made it through safely. I also prayed for my brother, Gerald, and his family. I spent most of my time just being thankful it was over with. I had planned to finish stacking things, but relaxed when I saw the daybreak and the sun.

And then all of a sudden, I heard sounds. It sounded like water was running. Just out of the blue, water was coming through the kitchen door. So I took the floor mat and put it at the bottom of the door and placed a storage cabinet in front of the door to keep some pressure on it. Then I started hearing the cracking of glass and I looked around. When I thought about it, the only glass that would be cracking would be the sliding glass door. When I moved the curtain back, I saw a crack creeping all the way up to the top of the glass. As I started stepping in water inside, I noticed the water was about six inches high outside. Water was coming from everywhere. I went to the front door and started to block it, but I said no and thought I had to be able to get out of here some kind of way. So I started getting some clothes and things together to pack a bag. The funny part about it was every time I packed a bag, it floated away. And I'm like "Where's the bag?" I'm in the back of the house and the bag is floating up to the front. I decided I needed to just put something on right fast. My shoes had floated away, so I put on jeans on top of the cutoff jeans I had on. I had a T-shirt so I put that on and I had a jacket so I tied that around my neck. But the only shoes I had were these steel-toe boots because the water couldn't push them around, so I put those on with no socks. I placed my wallet on the dresser, but when the dresser

flipped over, I lost my wallet and my keys and I had to go under water to get them. I put my belt around my neck. I found my sister's old twirling baton and took it in case I needed it. I said she must have left this for a reason, so if there's anything in this water, I am sure going to bat it in the head. I headed toward the front door. As I went through the house, I had to push everything aside, even the washer and dryer, just to pass by.

When I got to the front door, as I tried to open it the key dropped in the water. When I went to retrieve the key, I wasn't thinking, and my hat, belt, jacket, baton, everything floated from around my neck. The water was getting up to my chest. I pulled out the extra key in my pocket and used that to open the door. When you have water on both sides of the door, it's a struggle. When I did get the door open and looked outside, I started to close it back. The water was high out there—up to my neck. Then I thought, 'If I don't get out of here, it's going to be like that in here.' When I did get out, I tried to close the door but it was almost impossible. So the best I could do was close it with a little crack left in it, because by now the water was at my chin. Just a short time ago, the water was at my feet. Now it was at my chin. It had only been about 20 minutes.

I started bouncing up and down in the water. When I tried to start swimming, I wasn't able to because remember, I had the steel-toe boots on, so I had to swim under water and just fight my way back up. I aimed for my neighbor Carl's house and swam toward his truck, but the current pushed me pass it. When I came up next time, I grabbed the fence, stood on top, and held onto some trees while water rushed past me. The water was getting so high I had to decide where I was going to go. The first thing I did was to pray and ask God for His help, and I prayed, and I prayed, and I kept praying. I asked Him to forgive me for my sins, and for the ones I didn't

remember, and my prayer was, "Jesus, You say whatever we ask God in Your name You would give it to us, so God in the name of Jesus, I need help right now. I'm in trouble." He answered my prayers. By that time the water was at my chest as I stood on top a four-foot fence, a tire hit me in my back. While I was thanking Him for that, another tire came by and hit me on my right shoulder. That's when I started testifying, and I stand on this every day of my life. God does answer prayers. I looped my arms around the tires so I could float. Then I had to figure out where I was going to go.

I saw the old elementary school McDonogh #19, which is now renamed Louis Armstrong Elementary. It was the tallest building around. I got off the fence and pushed off as hard as I could so that the current would not carry me down our street. I had to duck under water while passing by the phone lines. When I got to the school, the current pushed me around it, so I kicked as much as I could to get back in that direction. When I got there, I stood on a 12-foot gate by the cafeteria. I was thinking I'd try and get to the roof by the cafeteria, but while I was standing there, a wooden bench came behind me and struck me in the back. When it hit me I fell off the fence and my leg fell over the outer portion of the gate. The fence was sticking me in my back and my leg was pinned between the gate and the bench. I lost one of the tires while trying to get my leg out. I had to go back to praying. I asked for the strength of Samson to help me get out of that situation because my leg was locked. It was beginning to look like I would be trapped. But I kept praying and kept praying. My legs were getting really numb so I knew I had to do something. That's when I pushed as hard as I could and my leg was released.

Now I had to figure out how to get out of that area.

With the one tire I had left, I pushed off with my right leg, because my left leg was still hurting. I headed toward the flagpole and ended up hitting the

fence, but at least now I had a chance to get to the front door of the school. I tried to keep the tire with me, but in the struggle to get it over the fence, I lost it, and I was exhausted to the point I couldn't pick it up. Meanwhile, another tree floated by and knocked me back into the water. I waited for the tree to pass and went back to getting back over the fence. I had to figure out what I was going to do next.

Having once been an electrician apprentice, I remembered that older buildings have electrical wiring on the outside. When I saw that I could hold onto the conduit wire, I anchored myself from the fence as I held onto the wire and walked the wall against the building. When I got to the front steps of the building, water had completely covered the first floor, but I was able to step onto the steps. I slipped on a step and hurt my back, but I thanked God for helping me to get up the steps and out of the water. When I got to the door of the building there was a big chain on the main door. I could tell immediately somebody was already in the building because the glass was broken on the side of the main door. I went in through the broken glass and as I entered the building, I saw dog droppings on the floor. I knew somebody was in there. I noticed the janitor had left a box of tools so I grabbed a monkey wrench and piece of pipe in case I needed protection and went straight up the steps to the secretary's office on the 2nd floor. I got a tablecloth that was on one of the tables in the hallway, and I left a crack in the door just in case I could hear anybody else. I also wrapped myself up because I was soaking wet and cold, and with the wrench in my hand I went to sleep knowing at least I was out of the water. Later on, the noise of the windows banging from the wind woke me up. As I was closing one window, it slammed down and busted my fingers. So now I was in more pain. On my way back to the office I heard somebody calling a dog's name. A woman

came down from the 3rd floor. She was with her kids and was calling for her dog. I told her I was down there by myself and asked if she minded if I came upstairs with them.

As I looked out the window on the 3rd floor, I could see people upstairs in another building close by trying to put out flags, and another man swimming down the street who joined us in our building. We all started scavenging for any food the teachers may have left behind in the building. We found milk and a little something to munch on so we initiated the honor code system: Take enough food to have something in your stomach, but don't eat everything up at one time. After I got something to eat, I went to hang a white flag on the front door.

It started getting dark. People passed by in boats taking pictures, but when we asked them for help, they told us they were with some kind of publishing company and the Coast Guard would be coming soon. It was disgusting. All these people were stuck and all they told us was that they were only there to take pictures.

It's nighttime now on that Monday. I found a big plastic bag to keep warm. Folks from the Coast Guard and different police departments came by in boats to pick up people. By that time, the Smith family, who had their own boat, had joined us. Their motor was broken, so they took one of the 20-foot pipes used for plumbing and used it like an oar to push them in the water. That's how we knew the water had gotten to 20-feet high. You couldn't see anything but the roofs of buildings, so being in the attic wouldn't have helped. I found out later that while I was praying outside my neighbor's house as I stood on top of the fence, he couldn't hear me because he and another neighbor were too busy praying inside of his house. They had been in the attic but fortunately they were able to get to a part of the house that had

a higher roof that they could stand on until they were rescued. That's why I said going into the attic wasn't a good idea at all.

Later that night a rescue boat came for us. We were letting the older people and kids get out first. One of the families said they weren't going to leave. The Coast Guard said the adults could stay, but they couldn't leave the kids. They had to take them with them. Eventually the family decided to go. From there, they brought us to the foot of the bridge so we could walk across. They also told us they were through for the night. One man I knew just had on some shorts, no shirt, and no shoes and was just laying there in the mud. I woke him up and he said, "I'm tired." I convinced him to get up and walk with me. I told him on the other side of the bridge is more help. "If you lay down here, you'll die," I said.

As we walked across the bridge, we saw more people and big Army trucks that were picking up families as they had room. I saw Fats Domino, legendary New Orleans musician, who lived not too far from our house. I said, "Hey, Papa Fats." And he says, "You think I can go home? I'm tired of this." I told him he can't go back. He said, "You think I can take a cab?" I laughed and told him yeah, if it's a boat cab. I told him if they had to have a boat to get him out, they're going to have to have a boat to get him back in. I told him everything was flooded. He said, "Everything?" I said, "Everything. We've got 20 feet of water." He said, "Even my house?" I said, "Even your house." That's when he started singing one of his famous songs, "Ain't That a Shame." When it came time for Fats and his family to be taken away, Fats tried to get me on with him, but they asked if I was family. Fats told him, "He's just like family." But they said only family could go. I told him, "That's alright, Papa Fats, I'll be okay." I sat down and waited. About two trucks later, I was able to get on.

When I got to the Superdome, I went straight to the 50-yard line and sat down where there was nobody around me. I fell asleep and when I woke up, the bag I had with me was empty and the shirt someone had given me was gone. There were a lot of people sitting around me and nobody saw anything. Then I realized … it really hit me. I'm here. Talk about struggles. There was so much confusion around. There were gangs walking around selling drugs and stealing. I heard that one little girl, and I don't know what her mama was thinking by letting her go by herself, I heard this little girl went to the bathroom and she was raped and killed in the bathroom. If somebody had an oxygen tank and their own people needed it, they grabbed it. If they had only gotten those buses and gotten people out, there wouldn't have been that mass exodus to the Superdome.

When the evacuation became mandatory, one thing was overlooked. There were many, many, many people in seven to nine low-income housing projects in the city. The smallest housing project had about 2,000 people and the largest had 10,000 people. Most of these people did not have cars and depended on public transportation to go to work and travel around the city. I think there should have been some assistance by means of the public transportation buses, school buses, or private or charter buses to take people out of the city. But that didn't happen, so a lot of people were stuck.

There was a lot of chaos in the Superdome. I think security should have traveled in three's, going in one direction toward the crowd, with another group of guards traveling in another section so they could stay in sight of each other. If they had done this, they could have curtailed and contained the crowd by circulating and constantly moving to make their presence known. Instead, they walked around in a group together and when that group passed, there was no security around, so all the evildoers would do was wait until that

group passed. It was chaotic. People were breaking into vending machines and selling drinks. One policeman went into the restroom and changed into his street clothes. He just gave it up on the spot.

One group fired a gun in the air. They had so many guns in the Superdome. So once they fired their gun, the other gangs said, "I've got a gun too," and Pow! Pow! Pow! All the guns started firing. People started running everywhere. Kids were knocked down. I got up on a table underneath the escalator and waited until things calmed down just a little. I thought maybe I should see if my mother was in the sports arena; this is where they moved those who were sick. I had missed two meals while looking for my mother and I was exhausted. I walked over there and told the guard I wanted to check to see if my mother was in there, and he let me in.

Over in the sports arena, things were all together different. Food and snacks were out where you could get to whatever you wanted and as much as you wanted. After being in the Superdome, I thought I had died and gone to Heaven.

I walked around and still didn't see my mother (I was told she probably went out with the first group to Houston), but I did run into Fats Domino again. He and his family were getting ready to board an Army airplane, so Fats told them to bring me along, too. But all of the seats were taken, and they said they couldn't take anybody else. He told me, "Take care of yourself." I told him I was alright—I'll be okay. Once again, I thanked him just for thinking of me and trying to get me out of this chaos. May God continue to bless him.

One man saw me talking to Fats and came over and started talking to me. I told him I was tired. I was looking for my mom and can't find her. He said, "I know man." He told me to take a seat in the section where he was in

charge and get some rest.

I went and found a seat in the sports arena to get some rest. I sat in the first row of seats and dozed off. I remember thinking I was a long way from home. I ended up talking to a couple sitting nearby all night. We didn't know who we were talking to until the lights came on.

That's when I got to see what really went down with the FEMA volunteers. All their buses backed up to the sports arena like a caravan. Nothing but a bunch of young, mostly white people came out with rolling travel bags and headed to the top to cross over to the Superdome. There were two or three lines of them, and they started throwing out food like they were in a Mardi Gras parade. People started running alongside the truck. When they saw that, and how people were acting, the next thing you saw were all those trucks and buses loading back up. They packed up and headed back out. They had never seen anything like that and they weren't about to deal with it. They turned around and packed up and got out. Do you hear me? Another thing that made it so bad was they should have sent experienced volunteers. This was a disaster, not a training session. When those young people saw how horrific things were, they couldn't handle it. I don't know if they were told to leave or if they made it up in their minds to leave, but whichever way it was, when they got to the front door of the Superdome, they turned right back around and left.

I think by now it's the Tuesday after the storm. I lost track of time. Days are running together. It's like a movie with no breaks and no pauses.

I went back upstairs to check on the patient rosters because I didn't physically see my mama. When I got there, they asked me if I needed to see a doctor. I said yes, because my back was still hurting from earlier when I'd slipped on the steps at the school, and my leg was still bothering me from

when the bench locked me up. My fingers were also damaged from the windows. I knew something was wrong because I felt the strain in my chest. They said if I wanted to see a doctor for myself I had to get in line and I could ask about my mama once I got written up as a patient.

Where they put me at the end of the line was outside the sports arena. I'd been inside. Now I had to start all over again. Once I went out there, it started to rain. I started to go back over to the Superdome, but my feet got stuck. I just couldn't go back over there. There were caravans of people steadily coming over to the Superdome from the third ward and walking through the water with their little belongings, all of them headed to the Superdome. People were acting all wild and I just couldn't deal with that. I said to myself, "I might as well stay here." There were kids outside in the rain, so I took a golf cart and got tape and cardboard and made a canopy, and then I let all the kids get in there to get out of the water. After I knew the kids were safe, I found a chair and some cardboard and put it over my head. I was just making the best of it.

I never did get back inside because the ambulances came to take sick people away from there. One little boy there, one of the kids I had helped get out of the rain, turned around and asked the ambulance personnel, "What about my uncle?" God bless him. And the ambulance people asked, "Is he with you all?" His mother said, "He's my son's uncle. He's been helping us all this time." So they said yeah, I could come. So that's how I got to get in an ambulance and that is how I got away from the Superdome: from the voice of a child who remembered me.

They took us to the airport and put me with the seriously ill. People were lying on the floor on paper, covered up, moaning and groaning, and throwing up. By now, my leg is swollen. I told them I still can function. I don't need to

be down here. So they sent me upstairs to another line.

When I got upstairs the nurse checked me and told me I needed to see a doctor. After I cleared that line to get into another line to see the doctor, who did I see again but the little boy and his mama. They were just like angels. May God continue to bless them.

From there I got on the plane—an Army helicopter that transports a bunch of people—and flew to San Antonio. They took us to San Antonio Kelly Air Force base and brought us to one of the office buildings that was being renovated. I found office chairs with wheels and started bringing them to all the older people: a lady whose walker had broken, a son who needed to push his daddy to the restroom, an older man, a lady with two children, and somebody sitting on the ground. One gentleman wanted to know why I didn't get him a chair. I said, "These are people that are worse off than you. I'm not doing it because I owe somebody something. I'm doing it out of the goodness of my heart." I told him if you've got enough strength to fuss at me, you've got enough strength to walk down and get a chair yourself. Everybody standing around said, "I know, that's right."

Once inside the office building, I went to the medical unit. The sad part about that was it was late, and the doctors were just giving people something to get through the night, so I couldn't get my prescription until the morning. I had been given a bed number, and sadness came upon me when I went to find my bed and they told me they gave it to someone else when they couldn't find me. I didn't have a place to lay my head. So I just walked to a back office and leaned against the wall. And that's when it hit me. All this time I had been trying to call my sister and couldn't get through. I realized I didn't have a way to get in touch with anybody. I didn't even have a place to lay my head. I became very tearful, and my heart was very, very sad. God bless the social

worker who came. I saw then that I had taken a seat in the social services area for people who were having mental problems. She saw I was full to the brim with grief, so she had compassion enough to tell me, "Look, you can sit here. You can go in this cubicle. A lady and her daughter were in one but you can go in this one right here. There should be a blanket in there. Just rest yourself." She told me don't worry about it. "God brought you this far, and you've been through what you've been through in the flood. He'll make a way for you." Then she said she heard people telling me thank you and saw me going back and forth getting chairs for those that needed. I told her I really just tried to do for people that couldn't do for themselves. God bless her. She gave me a cubicle with a fold-up cot and blanket, and that helped me make it through the night. The next morning, Wednesday, she came back and told me she had already told her manager about me, and as long as nobody else was using the cubicle, I could stay there.

I went to pick up my medicine and got a little something to eat. And when I came back, I kept noticing I couldn't get my slippers on. When I went to see about my feet, they took my blood pressure and found it was over 200. It was extremely high and that's why my feet were swelling. They told me if I had any belongings, tell them where they were and they would get them. Just don't move. I told them I didn't have but a few little things over there as I sat down and waited for the ambulance to come.

When the ambulance came, I got in and I was taken straight to the hospital. That's when I really got to have a good hot shower. Once I had a place to lay my head and get a shower, that's when I could really say, thank you Jesus, I must be in Heaven. I spent three or four days in the hospital. Time was running by so fast and I was steadily faced with obstacles, but I wasn't the only one. It was hard on everyone involved. At the hospital, I

entered my name and location in the database to get in touch with family members, and that's when I found out my sister had just recently put me on the list of missing persons. It was a coincidence that I spoke to the same person who spoke to her. She gave me the number and this time, the call went through, and that's how I was able to contact my sister to let her know I was in the hospital. Nine days had passed before I made contact with my family. Thank God for that. I made it to safety. From there, my brother-in-law's friend Ronnie picked me up from the hospital and took me to his house. He's a good person. God bless him. The next day he met my brother-in-law halfway and my brother-in-law brought me to Dallas. And that's my journey. From the water, to the hospital in San Antonio, and then to Dallas. I remember the Ninth Ward as a close community in New Orleans where everyone knew each other. The majority of families were established and you didn't have a great turnover of families moving in and out. If the house was rented, a lot of times it was rented by family members. There was a closeness that was unique in that people, to a certain point, continued to look after each other. It hadn't gotten to the point where what happened to others didn't concern me, but it was getting to be that way.

When I was very young, there were battles among the wards, but as I got older I found it was just economics and ignorance that divided the city. So New Orleans was beginning to get that craziness, and the Lord knows because that's why He washed it away. But it would not have been washed away that badly had some in charge not planned for it to be washed off only in certain areas of the city.

I've had extensive security training working with the school system and the Jazz and Heritage Festival, and I've been in the electrician's apprentice union and completed fireman's training. But the greatest job I enjoyed,

besides the money I made as a laborer on the riverfront as a sandblaster and the money I made as a plant operator at Kaiser Aluminum, was being a substitute teacher. I was able to go back to my former high school and teach and coach. Right now, I'm still looking forward to getting my song I wrote for the New Orleans Saints copyrighted. I want to make arrangements to sell it through an entertainment company and give the proceeds back to the city, as a gift for my life and my childhood. That's one thing I'd love to do, plus go to school to increase my culinary arts knowledge. I still look forward to writing a book about my horrific experience with the hurricane. I'll bring closure to my book by stating how life is a series of adjustments. I just acquired a new residence and I'm looking forward to being by myself because I need to develop and grow from the experience of feeling alone for 24 hours during the storm. I need to come to terms with my experience of nearly drowning in the storm, so the rooms being small will let me reap the benefits of meditation and solitude. I also look forward to substitute teaching again one day, along with improving my health. With this new place, I can at least walk around the block knowing I'm not far from having a place to sit down. Each day, I know I must do something that I enjoy doing. If not, it's not worth it. Money isn't going to make me any happier or my life any easier. Right now, after all I've been through, God has let me live through it all. There has to be a reason He has let me live, so I have to be very purposeful in all that I do.

PLAYGROUND

2117

Photo by Alexey Sergeev

Grace

"It was just time for Christians and for the Saints to do this (win the Super Bowl) because five years ago our city was almost wiped out. The Super Bowl win was to give us hope."

When we saw our house for the first time after Katrina, I was in shock. As we came across the bridge into the Lower Ninth Ward, I told my mom I wanted to go across the new bridge that had been built. But she said to look around. The new bridge is broken. So we had to come across the old rusty bridge.

I was so sad when we got to our neighborhood because I looked to the left and the house that was on the corner from our house wasn't there anymore. It was in the street. I wanted to run up the steps to our house, but my mom made me stop because the ground was full of mold and mildew and I could have easily slipped. I tried to walk, but I slipped and screamed. So my mom picked me up and carried me.

I asked my mom about Esther, our pet turtle. They joked and tried to make me feel better by telling me Esther was out of the tank now and could

breathe, and she was probably swimming in the water somewhere looking for some food.

Before Katrina, I remember we used to eat a lot of crawfish and shrimp and po-boys. We had lots of family that lived close by so we could get together real easily. That was nice. My daddy had a treadmill and I used to get on it and kick my feet up and swing. Another time, I was watching a Superman movie and felt so sad that he was dying. So I thought, 'What if I could be Superman or Supergirl?' So I stacked some boxes on the floor and jumped. I ended up breaking my arm and it was in a cast for eight weeks. All around the house I had memories of where I hurt myself trying different stunts.

The trip on the road to Dallas was really long. I asked my mom if we were ever going to get there. I thought Katrina was just another storm like all the other hurricanes. So I thought, 'I'm not worrying about this.' I did ask my mom, though, if we were coming back but she didn't give me an answer. When I saw the flood in New Orleans on TV at the hotel, I ran out the room and looked at my grandma, and she looked like she was devastated. I gave her a huge hug and told her it would be okay.

It's been hard for me missing stuff I loved, but new people reached out and gave us things, like a bunny named Star Grace and a jogging suit I like to wear. I wore it so much that when I tried to wear it again my mom would say, "No, you're not wearing that jogging suit again." I miss my Xbox. I wanted to bring it but we had so many people and clothes in the car, they said no, so I left my Xbox and my V.Smile learning system.

I've gotten used to my new environment. I've learned some people are nice, but they don't like to talk a lot. I miss our New Orleans food because it had a lot of spices. I just told myself I have to lower my expectations about the food. I've participated in the Dallas Children's Theatre and played

softball. I also am active in the Human Video project at church. I have new friends who are really nice.

If you've never been to New Orleans, you would really have a lot of fun. There's always something to do in the French Quarter and you can get free stuff. It has a lot of history. Some people have never been there and don't know our history and say our football team stinks and we don't care about our city. But they don't know we care about our city, and it was just time for Christians and for the Saints to do this (win the Super Bowl), because five years ago our city was almost wiped out. We're just getting started. The Super Bowl win was to give us hope.

Photo by Alexey Sergeev

Geraldine

"I was well known in the area because at one time I sold the Louisiana Weekly newspaper, insurance, and Avon. I knew every house in the Lower Ninth Ward from the Industrial Canal to Jackson Barracks."

My mom gave birth to me in Providence, Louisiana. Three months later she came back to New Orleans. My parents owned their home in the Lower Ninth Ward and I lived there for 83 years. It was the only place I ever lived before Hurricane Katrina.

Ours was a key lot on that block and the only house on the block facing our street. All the other houses on the block faced one of the other streets and backed up to our house.

I knew every house in the Lower Ninth Ward from the Industrial Canal to Jackson Barracks. I was well known in the area because at one time I sold the *Louisiana Weekly* newspaper, insurance, and Avon.

For 34 years I was also a librarian at a local university and also a missionary. I lived a beautiful life—a full life, including living in Africa for seven and a half years. I am very committed to my church, having raised $42,000 to replace church pews and bought 100 Bibles.

When I heard the storm was coming, my sister and I did what we did for every other storm: We called one of the local hotels and booked a room. We were at the hotel from Sunday until Tuesday. When the electricity went out, we went to stay at the Morial Convention Center for three days.

From there we drove to Houma, Louisiana, along with a friend. We didn't know a soul. Every place we tried was occupied, so we ended up staying with our friend's uncle, who took us in and let us stay with him for two months. After two months, we came back to New Orleans and stayed at a center that housed 16 or 17 other people for three weeks. I eventually ended up in a very nice retirement facility on the West Bank in Algiers. Before I moved there, I lived in seven other places. When there is a threat of hurricanes now, the facility takes us to a sister facility in Hot Springs, Arkansas, for safety. The Lower Ninth Ward has changed. There are few houses and only a few being rebuilt. The area is full of vacant lots and vacant blocks. You see more vacancies than homes. A lot of people are just unable to return. The Road Home program either didn't want to buy their home or they didn't qualify. I don't ever see it being the Ninth Ward we knew again. It's rough, real rough.

We lost everything in the storm, including 62 of my beautiful hats. The first time we went back to see the old house, my sister cried but I didn't. "The Lord giveth and the Lord taketh away," I said. Our next move is to Heaven.

Photo by Alexey Sergeev

Leatrice

"Dallas is not New Orleans, but we had no home. That's why we stayed here. We had no home."

It is amazing how God forged a friendship between two shy young college freshmen at Dillard University all those many years ago; this friendship has sustained us all our lives, even through Hurricane Katrina. I met my best friend Eleanor on September 17, 1945, at Dillard University in New Orleans. She was standing alone looking forlorn and from that point on, we just latched onto each other. Throughout our lives we have remained friends. My husband and I visited her when she lived in Mobile. I was in her wedding. We are very good friends.

When we evacuated New Orleans because of Hurricane Katrina, my family and I ended up in Paris, Texas, because that was the only place we could get a hotel reservation. After a couple of days in Paris, I called Eleanor, and she said she had been trying to call me. Eleanor said, "Girl I didn't know where you were. I'd been calling. You're not staying there." I told her I had my niece and her husband, my other niece with two boys and her husband,

and my husband with me. She said you can bring all of them. You come and stay here. That's how we ended up in a suburb of Dallas, Texas.

During Hurricane Betsy back in 1965, we left our house and stayed across the street at Southern University. By that time, we had moved from our home in the Lower Ninth Ward to a house in New Orleans East. I had my grandmother with me and my son was little, and my husband thought we should leave because flood waters were coming down Chef Menteur Highway not too far from our home. My son, mother, grandmother, husband, and my mother's neighbor, and I all stayed in one classroom at Southern. We would go back to the house periodically to get food, which we cooked there at Southern, but nothing happened to our home. There was no damage at all. We had been through so many other storms and never left for any of them, so when we heard Hurricane Katrina was coming, we were actually getting ready to go to church that Sunday morning when my husband's niece called and said they were coming to get us. My husband said "What?" and reminded them that I don't like to evacuate for hurricanes, so he didn't know about that. I told him we should be grateful that they invited us. Our son was away playing a gig so I know he was grateful that someone was thinking about us. I told my husband it was his call, so he said alright, we'll go. I thought we would only be gone a couple of days.

We drove in contra-flow lanes on I-10 out of the city. No one was coming the other way.

We stayed with Eleanor in Dallas a few weeks until October 2005 when we told her it was time for us to take off so she could get her life back together. We knew our home in New Orleans had to be demolished because it had been covered in six to seven feet of water. We had no furniture left. All I had left was some jewelry I found in my jewelry box. I kept the cheap

jewelry and the good jewelry in one box so if somebody broke in the house, they would think it was cheap jewelry and leave it alone. I was unable to find the earrings from my engagement in that box.

At that point we were homeless, so we thought we'd better find ourselves a new home. Eleanor took us to see some apartments for seniors and then we went to the Salvation Army and found some furniture and things for very little money. We stayed at those apartments until November before building a new home in a subdivision that was being developed. Dallas is not New Orleans, but we had no home. That's why we stayed here. We had no home. After Katrina, we had problems contacting insurance companies and waiting for inspections. We received enough money to live off of for a while until we could get things straightened out. My husband said it was a blessing that we both had retired and didn't need to look for jobs. The other thing was I had health problems, but because my health care coverage in Louisiana doesn't pay well in Texas, I had to return to New Orleans for an operation. I don't have Medicare because I had been a kindergarten teacher with the New Orleans School Board which did not offer it, and I couldn't get Medicaid because of my salary. Food is still a challenge as I still haven't gotten used to the different taste of food here in Texas.

I remember when I lived in the Lower Ninth Ward years ago the people who owned the slaughterhouse would give away leftover animal innards to the residents. All we had to do was bring our pots to put them in. People who had gardens gave produce away, not wanting to charge for everything like now. My grandmother made superb muffins, which she would take to different people in the church. One man from the church who was a fisherman would bring seafood and give it to others early in the morning. He gave us the best seafood at no charge.

Another one of my favorite memories of living in the Lower Ninth Ward was going to Macarty School and learning how to garden. One of the teachers had a garden for the kids to work on, and we would go to flower shows where winners were given trophies for different categories. The school had excellent gardens. I had a rose garden in New Orleans. I must say I'm happy here in Texas, even though I haven't seen many gardens like the ones at home. I like the open space here.

I was a kindergarten teacher, but I gave up teaching at one time to work for the Urban League to organize child development centers for underprivileged or low-income people. Residents from the community worked in the center and their children had to attend the center. After I left there, I went back to teaching.

I also have nice memories of my church, Amozion Baptist Church in the Lower Ninth Ward. I didn't have sisters or brothers, so the church was my extended family. When we moved here to Dallas I really enjoyed Eleanor's church, Antioch Fellowship Missionary Baptist Church, so my husband and I accepted the invitation to join. He is a member of the male chorus and I was invited to join the Mother's Board.

The people in the Lower Ninth Ward in my day were people who wanted a better life. They were industrious, creative, and they knew how to stretch a dollar because nobody had a lot of money. But we had what we needed. We may not have had the best built homes, but we believed in owning property, a car, and a house. We gardened to have food and took care of our mortgages. Katrina brought us to Texas and we've experienced many changes as a result. Katrina was devastating. Is it too much to bear? All I can say is through it all, the Lord has sustained us. Through it all, the Lord has provided.

Photo by Alexey Sergeev

Charles

"I decided to go back to the Lower Ninth Ward because I had no other place to go. I couldn't attempt to not come back, and once I got busy and started working and helping others in the community, I thought, "I'll just give it my all.""

When I heard Hurricane Katrina was coming, I thought we would be spared the brunt of it and would only have shallow street flooding. I figured we'd be back at home by the end of the week. But we all know what happened due to the failure of the flood wall.

My mom and I and her two cats left around noon that Sunday going to Birmingham, Alabama, to be with good friends who took me in for five weeks. My mom stayed in Birmingham until Thanksgiving.

On the way out of town, traffic was bad through Slidell, but then it opened up quite a bit and moved pretty swiftly. It took us about seven and a half hours to get there, which was about two hours more than normal.

It was major anxiety for us that first two weeks after Katrina. Then Hurricane Rita hit. That was our lowest point because we felt like now there was no way we could go back home.

People in Birmingham were very nice, very hospitable, and we were very thankful for that. They treated us to a lot of things and took us to different church services every weekend. Their support gave us a feeling of clarity and solidarity. I only brought three day's clothing with me when we left and people were very accommodating. Whatever we needed, they provided. I really appreciate all the people who helped us.

The first time I saw my house after Katrina—words cannot describe. My first indication that things were going to be horrific was what both my dad and his good friend told me the last weekend in September before I went home: "This is more than a notion. It's going take a while." I asked them if there was any place that was okay and they said uptown and Algiers. Both were fine. After that, I prepared myself to make the trek back. I got the necessary shots at a Birmingham clinic in case I stepped on a nail or something during my visit to New Orleans, and on October 9th, I left at 5 a.m. Friends from Atlanta met me and we caravanned to New Orleans.

When we reached Meridian, Mississippi, we could see a drastic change in the landscape. Trees and signs were uprooted. Wooden signs were snapped in half. I could see we were driving through the direct path of where the hurricane had been. We reached Slidell and it looked like bombs had gone off. In New Orleans East, where all the car lots had been, car lots were full of mud and debris. It kept getting worse and worse. People were on the side of the road crying and hollering.

There was only one radio station on and it played no music, just information on where to go for help.

When I reached the Lower Ninth Ward I could not get in. I had to wait for my dad who had a special pass for entrance. Guards checked you in at the base of the St. Claude and Claiborne bridges.

Once I entered the Lower Ninth Ward, words can't describe the mud and debris. Wood, doors—anything contained in a house—was out in the street. We had to be careful driving, because a lot of people got nails in their tires. We had to be out by 5 p.m. or the National Guard would order you to leave. Up until Christmas there were no lights, so most of the city, with the exception of downtown, uptown, and Algiers, was in total darkness at night, unless it was an area where they were able to get light poles back up quickly. For sure there were no traffic lights, only stop signs.

For Thanksgiving, I went to Birmingham to be with my mom. Leaving out of New Orleans and driving from Canal Street heading out, the rest of the way to Slidell was in total darkness. It was eerie. It was the first time I had seen that. It was a trying time.

I thought about staying in Birmingham after Katrina and even asked some people about jobs, but I found out that the university where I was administrator of the research center was not laying off and I still had a job. The university sent an e-mail to employees asking if they intended to come back and when and gave a cutoff date to respond.

On December 1st, I went back to work. We didn't have a lot of staff and three essential staff members were not back. I had to figure out how to divide up work until this person came back and that person came back, and figure out who would do this report, etc. One staff member said she had gotten settled where she was and found another job, and she wasn't coming back. This state of flux went on until Christmas. After Christmas, we hit the ground running.

We lost a lot of family pictures in the hurricane. Unfortunately, these pictures could not be salvaged. We lost old magazines that featured family members. I found out that my grandmother was in Ebony magazine in 1964.

All the articles were destroyed. None of our family members died during the storm, but afterward, we lost six relatives due to the stress.

I was able to recover things on the second floor of my house, but everything on the first floor had been destroyed. I was the only one in the family who had come back for a couple of months, so it was just me and my dad trying to clean up and throw out things at the house. He had bought the house back in 1980 when he got a really good deal on the home, and because of his involvement in civic and political affairs in the Lower Ninth Ward and eastern New Orleans, it was a good location for him. I followed in my dad's footsteps and am also very involved in the community. I decided to go back to the Lower Ninth Ward because I had no other place to go. I couldn't attempt to not come back, and once I got busy and started working and helping others in the community, I thought, "I'll just give it my all."

The house is back together now. It took three and a half to four years to finish it. While we were trying to rebuild, I had the anxiety of people coming to loot. A couple of times people did break into the house. We had the anxiety of making sure the house was properly boarded up until I could find a temporary location to put our things.

Once I came back, one of the challenges that we had was no grocery store in the area. We also needed a good quality pharmacy. The Lower Ninth Ward has changed. There are fewer people. We had a little over 17,000 residents before Hurricane Katrina. Now we have between 3,000 and 3,500. It is a little town within the city. I am very involved in the recovery of the Lower Ninth Ward and very active in my neighborhood association. I focus on helping the community recover with sustainable, energy-efficient housing and helping other family members and friends get jobs. There is a constant barrage of requests for resources.

What I want people to know is that those who are back in the Lower Ninth Ward are resilient, committed to the neighborhood, and trying to be as energy-efficient as possible. We are also working on bringing in a pharmacy, another school, and a grocery store. And with only 3,200 residents, we have 23 churches open. Our faith is alive and well.

Photo by Alexey Sergeev

Evelyn

"I know that I may never return home but I will always love New Orleans. I still have fond memories of my neighbors and the closeness we shared in the Lower Ninth Ward."

One of my vivid memories of living in the Lower Ninth Ward is buying records from the record man who drove through the neighborhood in his truck. He had all the latest hits for 50 cents. All you had to do was hum the tune and he knew the song. In fact, a lot of services came right to your front door, including sewing material, insurance, home interior products, and Avon.

My parents moved to the Lower Ninth Ward and purchased the same house where I was living when Hurricane Katrina struck. They owned a business and were married for 15 years before I, their only child, was born. Maybe my dad decided not to have a large family because he had 20 brothers and sisters. I have more than 250 first cousins. I lived in the Lower Ninth Ward for all of my life until Katrina and Rita struck. I attended Alfred Lawless Elementary and Junior High schools in the Lower Ninth Ward. I am a graduate of McDonogh #35 High School. I received my college education:

A B.M. in music education, piano major/voice minor, and an M.A in education from Xavier University of Louisiana. Unlike reports of everyone being poorly educated and on welfare in the Ninth Ward, my family and many other families worked hard to educate their children and promote a positive family life.

Before Katrina, I worked for the State of Louisiana as a rehabilitation counselor and a church musician. Being a musician included lots of public contact and travel. Before the storm, I was able to pay off bills and remodel my home. I got to enjoy my remodeled home for only six months before Katrina came.

When I heard that Hurricane Katrina was imminent and heard the mayor and governor on TV being so indecisive, I decided that I was leaving the city. A lot of people stayed. Some of my neighbors died staying there in their homes. Many had lived in the area for more than 20 years or so. The last time it flooded was in 1965 with Hurricane Betsy. The way the water came in from Hurricane Katrina was like a tsunami. Many persons including myself believed the levee system built after 1965 was sufficient enough to hold back the flood waters. Hurricane Katrina swept up houses in a wave, and just picked them up and threw them down. I still wonder what happened to many of my neighbors. Some nearby neighbors were found dead in their homes and others may never be found.

When I left New Orleans that Sunday before Katrina hit, I headed to Clinton, Louisiana, which is one hour from Baton Rouge. My dog and I were in traffic for nearly 12 hours. When I reached Clinton, I lived with my aunt and cousins for a year in her home and then in a FEMA trailer that was placed on her property. Then, a family friend told me about a house being built on one and a half acres on a corner lot with three bedrooms and two and a half bathrooms that was in my price range. I was sold. The area

is very quiet and peaceful. I have a very large family in Clinton and my job transferred me to the area, so I decided to make Clinton my new home.

Based on the stories I have heard, it sounds like I did not have it as hard as most people. Since I was employed by the state, my salary continued until I was placed in a more suitable work location. All state employees had direct deposit, so income was not interrupted. I had money for food, shelter, and clothing. Not everyone was so lucky. Many persons lost their jobs in addition to their homes. Many families were pulled apart. I did have problems proving past transactions that had taken place due to important papers being lost in the hurricane. I had to get a great deal of information recreated. It has also been difficult being in a new location and getting used to the drive. In New Orleans I drove six miles to work. Now I drive 33 miles, some on a two-lane highway.

Another challenge right after the storm was not knowing what you had left in your house or if you had a house to go back to at all. I was not permitted in the Lower Ninth Ward until late November 2005 because of the extensive damage in the area. This was the worst feeling anyone could have to see not only a city destroyed, but your own neighborhood. The Ninth Ward was not recognizable due to the extent of the destruction. Many homes were no longer standing and some were never found. On Reynes Street, where I lived all my life, my house was standing with most everything inside destroyed. I saved what I could but I knew that I could never call it home again. I sold my home in 2008 to the Road Home program.

It's different now in the Lower Ninth Ward. There's a different atmosphere there. I know that I may never return home but I will always love New Orleans. I still have fond memories of my neighbors and the closeness we shared in the Lower Ninth Ward.

Photo by Alexey Sergeev

Gabrielle

"The first time it really hit me as to what had happened was at a dinner for Katrina survivors. Someone was ministering to us and preaching when my older sister and I just started crying. It hit us then that this is really true. It felt like a dream—no, a nightmare."

It snowed in New Orleans for the first time I can remember in 2004. I kept telling my mom it was going to snow and kept going to the front door checking. I stood by the door the whole time. When the snow did start, I ran and told everybody. My cousins and I, along with everybody from the neighborhood in the Lower Ninth Ward, were outside laughing and throwing snowballs. That was the year before Hurricane Katrina.

Before Katrina, life was very family oriented. We were living with my grandmother in the Lower Ninth Ward and somebody was always at home. The house was never quiet. We would see our family all the time. We didn't need a family reunion because everybody came by, especially around Thanksgiving and Christmas. We had two kitchens. We had everything we needed.

I remember how sweet everybody in New Orleans was. When you walked

down the street, you spoke to everybody, especially the elderly. Everyone was nice and generally friendly.

When I heard the hurricane was coming, I have to admit I really didn't take it seriously. I treated it like all the other hurricanes—a vacation. I took four outfits and a CD player to listen to in the car for what I knew was going to be a long drive. Hurricane Ivan had just hit and that was a two-hour drive. The hurricane was just another opportunity to get out of town and get out of school. With Ivan, we stayed in Baton Rouge and saw family we hadn't seen in a while. We laughed and played poker and other card games. We knew the hurricane was going to hit on Monday, so we left New Orleans on Sunday. We figured we'd be back on Tuesday.

We headed toward Shreveport to stay in a hotel in Bossier City. It was not as much fun as it had been before. In a big van, Katrina was scarier, and we could feel the winds and rain as we were driving. As we were leaving, I wasn't thinking about the hurricane, though. I was talking to my parents and listening to the weather on the radio.

I remember exactly where I was when I learned the hurricane had hit. We were in Bossier City. It was 7 a.m. on Monday, and I was sitting on the floor in mama's room when I saw that the Food Mart not far from my grandmother's house on TV flooded. It was the first place I saw on TV, and it was sitting in water and everything was covered. I felt like I was in shock, like somebody from the family had died. My grandmother was lying in her bed surrounded by tissues, crying.

The first time it really hit me as to what had happened was at a dinner for Katrina survivors, which was held at my aunt's church in Dallas. Someone was ministering to us and preaching when my older sister and I just started crying. It hit us then that this is really true. It felt like a dream—no, a nightmare.

It was difficult coping with my new life. I begged my mom not to make me go to the new school. I wanted my old school and my old friends. I remember sitting in my new middle school principal's office with my eyes tearing up as they talked about registering me for classes. I've met lots of new friends in Dallas and I am adjusting. I played on the softball team and was even voted homecoming queen. I'll be studying pre-law in college this fall. It didn't matter as much to me losing the material things. I miss things with sentimental value more. It hurt that I lost my MVP trophy from my first year playing glove ball and competing in the Louisiana Babe Ruth Softball State Tournament as a member of the Lakeshore All-Star team. Playing on that team had given me confidence in myself. It would be good to still have that trophy. I miss Kenilworth Park where we used to play our recreation softball games and Lakeview where we played our all-star games. My brother says the park is not the same anymore because there are different coaches and different kids. We would go there to hang out, even if we weren't playing. We'd eat hamburgers and watch the others play.

I remember a baby picture of me we used to have. I was either one or two years old and I was standing with a blanket wrapped around me with my small face and chubby cheeks. I may have had a pacifier in my mouth. We don't have that picture anymore or any baby pictures of me I can think of. I'd like people to know that you may see Mardi Gras and the news reports of corruption in New Orleans and voodoo. It's true we do have those things, but there is also a beauty and love and care that a lot of cities don't have. New Orleans people are open and friendly. Other places are not as friendly. If you could have seen it before Katrina, you would see a different side: Not everyone is needy or acting crazy. There are a lot of good people in New Orleans. There were some people in my new school who were from

New Orleans who seemed to have no common sense; I thought, "Who are these people?" They are not the people I knew in New Orleans nor do they represent the people of New Orleans. People saw only the bad in the news. Before you judge, think how you would feel if everything you had was flooded and you had no control over it. See how you would feel.

Photo by Alexey Sergeev

Illona

"When I saw the images on TV of the flooding and destruction, one of my first thoughts was, 'What about my dogs?' Every time I saw a commercial on TV about dogs or dog food, I felt so awful and just curled up in silence."

Five years after Hurricane Katrina and my life just now seems like it's getting back on track. Just the fact that I live in a city I didn't know and was not planning to visit, made me feel like I had no control over my life. When all of this happened, I felt like the rug had been pulled out from under me. I liked the life I had in New Orleans prior to Hurricane Katrina. I worked full time in graphic design and I was also a sign language interpreter at the junior college and one of the universities. I was in school full time and very focused on getting my master's degree in special education in order to reach my goal of teaching deaf individuals. But Katrina threw a monkey wrench in my plans. When Katrina hit, I was in my last year of school.

I actually lived in the Lower Ninth Ward twice. I was raised in the house my parents bought in the Ninth Ward when they married. My mom used to grow mint in the alleyway and she would make mint tea for us when we had

a tummy ache. My brothers and I would catch lightning bugs, look at water moccasins, and dig for earthworms to go fishing.

Growing up, the Ninth Ward was more like a family. Even if you didn't know a person, you looked out for each other. Even though people said it was dangerous, we felt safe. It was very family oriented. We walked from house to house. Friends walked to school.

I remember being in dance school, music, and art classes. For a short time I took piano lessons from Mrs. Dolliole. My family kept me involved in band at Lawless Junior High and McDonogh #35 High School. Our band instructor, Lloyd Harris, and the band helped keep me together. I played B-flat clarinet and was starting to learn a little about playing some of the other instruments such as the flute, bassoon, and saxophone. Music was soothing and comforting to me.

As an adult, I moved back to the Lower Ninth Ward and rented a house. I really liked that house with the green paneling and thick grass on the lawn. This house was in a very quiet neighborhood. I liked looking out of my kitchen window and enjoying the peace while I washed dishes. Six years prior to Katrina, I had purchased a home on the West Bank.

When I heard Katrina was going to hit, I said "Oh no, not again." I really didn't want to leave, and thought it probably won't be too bad. The last time I left for a hurricane, I took my dog and her eight newborn pups with me and we stayed in a motel. I ended up spending money I didn't have to spare. But some friends convinced me that I didn't need to stay there by myself for Katrina, so I left on Sunday.

When I left New Orleans for Katrina, I did not take my three dogs with me. I figured we'd just be gone for a few days, so I left them inside the house with plenty of food and water and newspaper. My thought was to protect

them from any flying debris that could be caused by high winds. When I saw the images on TV of the flooding and destruction, one of my first thoughts was, "What about my dogs?" I listed them on every website I could find that helped Katrina survivors reconnect with their pets. Every time I saw a commercial on TV about dogs or dog food, I felt so awful and just curled up in silence. I was worried. Were they alright? Were they starving? Were they dead? It turns out they were rescued and placed in shelters—two in one shelter and one in another. It took me two months to get the first dog and three months to get the other two. I am really grateful because an animal rescue volunteer worker called me from each of the shelters to let me know that my dogs were safe and where I could go and get them. A friend and I made two trips to go and get them. The drive to get the first dog took about eight and a half hours one way; the second trip was a little shorter, taking approximately five hours. I was so happy to see them. There would be a big hole in my heart if I were to lose them.

It was such a struggle trying to get the info I needed from the mortgage company while trying to hold onto my house on the West Bank at the same time. For five years, I tried everything—attorneys, legal aid—but I was not able to find anybody to take an interest in my situation. I sent letters to the mayor and others. Living in another city, I felt like I had no options. It still gets hard emotionally sometimes. I used to be a homeowner and now I'm not. The home is not my property anymore. The mortgage company took it over and I have nothing. Once I was left without a home in New Orleans and with very little chance of getting a decent paying job in my field, I felt like it would have been a step backward to return. The places where I used to work were closed due to severe storm damage, and there was no guarantee of work and a full-time job.

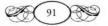

I am now working full time as an American Sign Language interpreter and teaching assistant to deaf and hard-of-hearing high school students, which I really enjoy. I finally finished my master's degree and am working toward becoming a teacher and getting state certification to teach sign language classes. I have also applied for an alternative certification program. I would actually like to start teaching English as a second language to deaf students and also to students of other language backgrounds. I was without transportation for a while, but my church recently blessed me with a car. My daughter, who was in high school when we left New Orleans, is now a sophomore in college.

Sometimes it bothers me not being in my own home. Eventually, I would like to get back to being a homeowner. Things are getting better and I'm praying that continues. I'm making progress.

Photo by Alexey Sergeev

Clara Mae

"Some of my favorite memories are relaxing and playing games with kids in the neighborhood. It was peaceful and everybody looked out for everybody else. I would come home from work and find a houseful of kids doing homework."

My life before Hurricane Katrina centered around my family: my husband, our sons, and their kids. I was an assistant housekeeper at one of the hotels and we were planning to open a family landscaping business. I was born and raised in New Orleans and owned my home in the Lower Ninth Ward. I was happy and content. Some of my favorite memories are relaxing and playing games with kids in the neighborhood. It was peaceful and everybody looked out for everybody else. I would come home from work and find a houseful of kids doing homework. Saturday and Sundays were family time. Everybody would gather for Sunday dinner.

When I heard Hurricane Katrina was approaching, I thought we were going to die. I saw how big it was, and I knew we were not supposed to stay. I feel sorry for those who stayed. I know many of them had no way to go and couldn't leave.

I told my employees to go home, and I left to go home myself about 11 a.m. Sunday. Fortunately, my sons had done a lot of the packing, so I rushed to put together what I could. We gathered some important papers and the 15 of us hit the highway about 2:30 p.m. Traffic was stop and go and some intersections were blocked. We had enough gas, but decided to stop and get gas where it wasn't so crowded and not as much traffic. We stopped at one gas station and people were fighting over gas, so we went on to the next one. When we arrived at my cousin's house in Houston, she helped us get settled in a hotel where we stayed for about a week. Then some of my co-workers called and said they had been trying to reach me. They had rooms for us at a hotel in Houston that was a part of the hotel chain where we worked. We stayed there until November 2005.

The first time I saw my house after Katrina, I had a nervous breakdown. The house was turned sideways. If it had not been for the light pole, the entire house would have washed away. Out of eight houses on our block, only two remained.

We lost all kinds of pictures in the storm—baby pictures and pictures of my son in the Navy. We're thankful we didn't lose anybody.

We decided to rebuild, but it was hard to get supplies and other stuff we needed like financial aid. We didn't know which way to go. I had never been through devastation like this.

I knew that me and my husband would be okay after Katrina, so my prayer was for the children to get stable once again in New Orleans. I just wanted to make sure my grandkids were okay.

When I came back to New Orleans, my husband was not working and we had to keep an income, so I worked but I worked fewer hours. I was just getting back on my feet when I lost my job, and we were just starting our

landscaping business. It was very stressful. The good thing about it was with the time off I was able to take care of the business. We got a trailer and placed it on my cousin's property, but after a while we had to move the trailer. In April 2006 we moved into a trailer on our property, and we moved into our home in 2007, using money we received from Road Home.

Now, some days are good and some days are bad. It's depressing to live in an area where the grass is not cut, and there's not all the activity from residents like there was before. I worry about my son who drives a cab. I thank God for the good days. When I hear about hurricanes approaching now, I do what I've always done. I leave.

Photo by Alexey Sergeev

Celestine

"Everyone knew each other. Sometimes you couldn't tell who were blood relatives and who weren't. Everyone was like family. That's why I had to come back here."

We left New Orleans the Friday before Hurricane Katrina so we could get an early start on traffic. We knew traffic was going to be bad. Not too long before Katrina, we fled the city because of another hurricane, and the drive to Baton Rouge that should have taken us an hour and a half took 18 hours. We did not want to go through that again.

When we left New Orleans I only brought a change of clothes for two days, an insurance policy, some other important papers, and some papers for our 50-year high school class reunion, which had been set for the weekend before Katrina. We also brought pictures of my mom and daddy and a saint statue that had belonged to my grandmother. This was just a weekend vacation, right? And we were happy for the break. We had no idea things would turn out like they did.

There were 19 of us leaving New Orleans heading to Jackson, Mississippi, including my three children, five grandkids, my daughter-in-law and her two

sisters, and their seven children. When we couldn't find a place in Jackson, we ended up in Montgomery, Alabama. From there, we moved to Natchitoches, Louisiana (the oldest city in Louisiana) for a month trying to find a place to live. At this time our group decided to separate. Shortly thereafter, one of my relatives came looking for me and we decided to move to Alexandria, Louisiana, where we stayed with a relative for two months.

When we got ready to move from my relative's house in Alexandria, the Lord was looking out for us. We were riding and looking for a house when I saw a big house with a large yard ideal for my grandchildren. The owner drove up and asked us what we were doing. I told her we were looking for a place to stay. She told us the house was not for sale or rent and she drove off a short distance, but then she came back and asked for my name and phone number. She worked at the hospital across the street from the house. The next day she called me and told me that the Lord told her to let me have the house and that we could move in and she would not charge us rent the first month. There were some nuns living two doors down and they brought over clothes, blankets, toiletries, sheets, towels, and games for the children. They also brought food and baked cookies, air beds, and chairs. The house already had a refrigerator and stove. People were really nice to us. By this time, there were only 10 of us, four adults and six children, and I stayed in that house for a year. It was nothing but the Holy Spirit interceding for us, because we had been looking for a large house for days.

I retired from the St. Bernard Parish Schools where I taught math and special education. Before Katrina, I took care of my husband and my sister. My husband died a year before Katrina, and my sister after that. Most of my time was spent going to church, being involved in community activities, teaching Sunday School, and working with the youth group.

My favorite memories of the Lower Ninth Ward are the friendships I

developed. I was born in the Lower Ninth Ward. Everyone knew each other. Sometimes you couldn't tell who were blood relatives and who weren't. Everyone was like family. That's why I had to come back here. I love my home and the neighborhood. I had no desire to start over.

The flood waters from Hurricane Katrina crashed over the top of my house. I had the same problems with contractors as everybody else in trying to get my house repaired. People signed with them and they didn't complete the work, plus they overcharged. I started keeping an eye on my materials and bought my own. The house still isn't finished, but it's livable.

The neighborhood still has not come back. A lot of our neighbors have passed away and the property was left to their kids who either tore down the house or boarded it up. And there is no shopping nearby. We still have to drive to St. Bernard Parish to buy groceries or to Metarie or across the river to go shopping. They did build a new three-story home for senior citizens a few blocks from my house, though.

I regret losing my kids' baby pictures, notes I kept from my students, and CDs, sheet music, and music books I had collected. We also lost our family pets in the storm—two birds and a dog.

I'm still active in my church and the community, but now I also play basketball with the Silver Slammers, a basketball group for women ages 65 plus in New Orleans. And we're good! We participated in the National World Games Silver Olympics for the past two years and brought home gold and bronze medals. Playing keeps me active and my mind occupied. Plus, I really enjoy it.

One thing Hurricane Katrina did was help me realize the abundance of stuff we had around the house. So many clothes and things that we really didn't need. I try to live more simply now. My family survived the storm and I have good health, so we're okay.

Photo by Alexey Sergeev

Almeaner

"Hurricane Katrina turned our world upside down. Imagine having to start over when you're almost 70."

I thought my life was all set. After retiring from the telephone company in 1999, me and my husband, who worked for New Orleans Public Schools, were ready to enjoy retirement. We were ready to enjoy it because we had planned for it. We examined our monthly income and bills and felt we could handle it all and live in comfort. I could even take a cruise or two and enjoy the grandkids. We thought that the way our life was then was the way it would be for the rest of our lives.

Hurricane Katrina turned our world upside down. Imagine having to start over when you're almost 70. And not just lose a lot of things—lose everything. The hardest things to lose were the pictures and mementos—my daughters' wedding pictures, baby pictures, pictures of loved ones who had passed on, and videos of birthday parties. Things you can never replace, all down the drain. I relocated to Dallas for a few years after Hurricane Katrina, but I decided to move back to be near family. I knew I wouldn't always be as mobile as I am now and I may not be able to travel to New Orleans to visit.

My cousins are my age and soon they won't be able to travel either, so we can see each other. I wanted to be back home.

Instead of moving back to the Lower Ninth Ward, I moved to the West Bank, which was much less affected by the storm. A lot of people moved to the West Bank after Katrina, hoping they would find the same shelter and solace should another hurricane descend upon us. Lots of other people felt the same way, thus making the area a lot more crowded than it was before Katrina. It's different from the Lower Nine, but at least we have all the conveniences nearby. One of my daughters lives not far from the Lower Ninth Ward and she has to drive to Metairie to find a grocery store. Two of my daughters have returned home and I was hoping the third one would as well. But she has school-aged children, and I knew she wouldn't move back until the school system was in order.

There isn't any place like the Ninth Ward. Everybody knew everybody, if not by name then by face, and was always willing to help if needed. On a postal worker and practical nurse salaries, my parents bought the big double house where we lived in the early 1950s. I was a freshman in high school and my sister was a sophomore.

It was a large family house with five bedrooms and three full bathrooms. My parents lived on one side and my family lived on the other. After my parents died, I bought out my sister's half of the house and just me and my family lived there.

We left that Sunday afternoon before Hurricane Katrina hit. Thinking we would only be gone a couple of days, just like we had before, we headed to Bossier City to spend a couple of nights in a hotel. When I woke up Monday morning and saw the pictures of New Orleans on TV, I felt numb. New Orleans didn't even look like a city. All you could see were the tops of trees. Not able to return home and unable to stay in a hotel indefinitely, we sought

refuge in the home of close family friends in Dallas. They assured us we had a place to stay. They opened their hearts and their home. They prepared a place for us and made us feel comfortable. They changed their living room into a dormitory filled with bunk beds. Their neighbors and church provided food and offered emotional support. I don't think they realize what they did for us. I didn't go back home to see the house for myself until the following January, but I saw pictures before then. When I saw pictures of what used to be our beautiful family home, I broke down and cried.

I worry about my grandkids and how this experience has affected them. They were uprooted and had to learn how to live in a different place and go to different schools. I know it's hard to be the new kid on the block. I pray they have no residual effects from the experience.

Looking at TV and reading the newspapers, you would think that everyone who lived in the Ninth Ward was poor, didn't own their own home, and had no transportation, and that's just not true. Everybody in our neighborhood owned their homes, with the exception of people who lived in the apartment complex down the street.

One day while living in Dallas, I was at my physical therapist and I overheard two ladies talking about how people from New Orleans were "getting over" and had "made out like bandits" with all the government aid they received from Hurricane Katrina. I had to stop and ask them what did they think we were getting? I told them they should be in my shoes for two weeks. I was blessed because we did not lose any loved ones, but my kids and their husbands have no jobs. Some had no place to stay, and no one helped them. We don't have pictures of our kids and our parents. I would give back any aid we received to get back what I lost. I told them, "Sweetheart, I would not wish this on my own worst enemy."

Meet The Author

Award-winning writer Lynette Norris Wilkinson was born to write. From the time she won her first writing contest at the age of 11, she has always sought self-expression through writing that inspires, influences, and informs. Job titles may have changed over the years, but she considers herself first and foremost a writer. She feels she did not arrive at this point in her life by accident. Her journey has been filled with peaks and lows, roundabouts and sidetracks. Each new job, location, challenge, and experience was perfectly orchestrated to bring her to the exact spot where she is today.

Born and raised in the Lower Ninth Ward of New Orleans, she attended Macarty School (kindergarten), McDonogh #19 Elementary School, Lawless Junior High School, and McDonogh #35 Senior High School. At her elementary school in New Orleans, her sixth grade teacher encouraged her to write poems and essays. She entered contests in the local paper and won. For her efforts, she received a stuffed animal and a little cash. From that, she learned the value of the written word.

After graduating cum laude from Texas Southern University in Houston, Texas, with a major in journalism and a minor in marketing, she took a

job with Dun & Bradstreet as a business reporter. She gathered financial information from business owners and talked to them about the structure of their businesses. Some welcomed her visit. Many did not. Regardless, she picked up the phone or drove to the next business and moved on to the next company on her list. She learned about business, and balance sheets, and budgets—and perseverance.

After marrying and moving to Dallas and working in customer service for a publishing company for a few years, she decided she wanted to get back into writing. Lynette volunteered with the Dallas Public Library and other nonprofit agencies and wrote articles, brochures, and manuals to build her portfolio. She had learned how to reinvent herself.

This really worked in her favor because she was later hired as a technical writer. When Lynette found herself without a job in the aftermath of 9/11, she applied with a major health system in Dallas for a job as a public relations coordinator. The director at that time was not looking for someone with public relations experience; she just wanted a strong writer. That fit Lynette perfectly because she saw where she could use her technical, creative, and business background. She learned it was possible to have a job that fits her personal style and talents, plus work with wonderful people.

In August 2005, Lynette found herself with 16 family members and friends on her doorstep when Hurricane Katrina struck New Orleans. They had nothing but the clothes on their backs and the few possessions they had in their cars. But they had their lives, and they had each other. Through this experience, Lynette learned what really matters.

Seeing the devastated Lower Ninth Ward, she had the God-inspired idea to write a book that celebrated hurricane survivors from that area and donate the proceeds to organizations that are helping residents recover. She says,

"You see me as I am now, but there was where it all began. These are my roots and my people. How could I not use my gift to do what is within my power to help?"

And so the book, UNTOLD: The New Orleans 9th Ward You Never Knew, was born. The author says, "If this is the best and biggest thing I ever do in my life, I will be happy."

ODE TO THE LOWER NINTH WARD

By Lynette Norris Wilkinson

We almost washed away.
Our homes, and our families, and the corner stores and the barrooms,
And the hospitals and the schools, and the churches, and the restaurants,
We almost washed away.
Waters washed away families and generations, and keepsakes and heirlooms,
And pictures and cars and furniture.
And mingled them with tears.
We almost washed away.
Still trying to come home and rebuild, with one neighbor maybe two,
And weeds and vacant lots where a neighborhood once stood.
We almost washed away.
Where are our people and the laughter and the kids playing,
And the smiles and the waves?
Where's my grandma's house and my auntie's house? Where's my grandma?
We almost washed away.
BUT,
The memories remain, unstoppable and invincible
As the warmth of remembrances from happier times brings joy to the soul
When all is washed away,
The playback in our minds glistens brightly in the sun
Where there is no mud and flood and mildew and rotting bodies,
And raise high above the sky soaring into the heavens,
Where no man's touch can hurt us anymore.

To order additional copies of this book, visit;

www.HurricaneKatrinaStories.com

www.Amazon.com

www.BarnesAndNoble.com

UNTOLD

THE NEW ORLEANS 9TH WARD
YOU NEVER KNEW

LaVergne, TN USA
04 November 2010
203528LV00002B/2/P